MUSTANG WING

RAF Brenzett
Advanced Landing Ground

Romney Marsh, Kent
1942-1944

by
Anthony John Moor

First published in 1999

British Library Cataloguing in Publication data
A Catalogue record of this book is available from
the British Library.

ISBN 0 9531421 1 6

Published and Printed by
HPC Publishing, Drury Lane, St Leonards-on-Sea,
East Sussex TN38 9BJ, England
Telephone: (01424) 720477

Also produced by HPC Publishing:

British Aircraft at War 1939-45
by Gordon Swanborough

Front Cover:
'Watching Station' by Ivan Berryman. North American Mustang IIIs of No 315 Polish 'Deblinski' Sqn on fighter cover duties above the invasion fleet on D-Day, June 1944. The nearest aircraft is FB166, the personal mount of the squadron's Commanding Officer, Capt Eugeniusz Horbaczewski.

Contents

Sqn Ldr E Horbaczewski, CO, No 315 (Polish) Sqn, Polish Air Force, killed in action on August 18, 1944, flying from Brenzett ALG, from a painting by a close friend and fellow pilot. (T. Slon).

Author's Preface

As a member of Brenzett Aeronautical Museum Trust, I became interested in the brief but fascinating history of the wartime Advanced Landing Grounds, about which little seems to have been written. In particular, the airfield close to the museum caught my attention. This book is not a complete history of ALGs, but I was fortunate to obtain the first-hand stories from pilots, ground crew and civilians who served or lived on Romney Marsh during the hectic summer of 1944, when Mustangs of No 133 Wing, 84 Group, took off from the ALG at Brenzett to intercept V1 flying bombs, and provide air cover and support for the invasion forces after D-Day.

I have received help from many sources including, in particular, those who are mentioned below. I hope the reader will enjoy this 'peep through the hedge' at an almost forgotten airfield.

Sqn Ldr T Andersz DFC; J Bargielowski VM, CofV, DFM; T P Barnes; Brenzett Aeronautical Museum Trust; R Chapman; Sqn Ldr M Cwynar VM, KW, DFC; G R Dickson; S Dzialowski; A Grodynski; Sqn Ldr L K Grzybowski AFC; P Hamlin; F Holmes; M Humphries; R Huntsman; F Jarvis; Z Jelinski; Kent Aviation Historical Research Society; T J Krzystek; A C Leigh; Sqn Ldr L G Lunn; Museum of Army Aviation; P Nickolson; Dr B J A Nowosielski-Slepowron; H J Pietrzak VM, CofV, DFC; J Polak VM, CofV; Polish Air Force Association; The Polish Institute; Public Records Office; G Pyle; RAF Association; J B Siekierski; T Slon; W Smith; K Stembrowicz; M Tanner; A Thomson; Sqn Ldr P D Thompson DFC; P Warman; P Wass; I G Wood; A E Wright; K Wunsche; M Young; J Z Zulikowski.

Introduction

Among the more elderly visitors to the Brenzett Aeronautical Museum Trust – situated close to the Romney Marsh villages of Brenzett and Ivychurch – many memories will be stirred by the sight of the remains of a V1 on display. Few among them, though, may be aware, as they gaze across the flat expanse of the local landscape, that 50 years and more ago, a busy airstrip was located within earshot of today's museum.

Better known locally as the Ivychurch Airstrip, it was officially Brenzett Advanced Landing Ground (ALG). From it, aircraft of the RAF rose to meet the threat of the V1s, which first struck Britain on June 13 and continued to arrive in large numbers during the summer months of 1944.

As early as July 1942, Brenzett had been identified as a suitable site for an airstrip, on the recommendation of the Aerodrome Board. Detailed planning and formalities to requisition the land were set in motion. To stabilise the two grass runways needed, a type of steel mesh surface, known as Summerfeld Tracking, would be laid. Four blister hangars were to be erected, while accommodation would be provided in tents; in addition, Moat House and its surrounding buildings, located on the eastern side of the proposed airstrip, would be requisitioned. Tons of rubble from bomb-damaged cities were transported to the area for the construction of Brenzett, and other planned airstrips. Civilian workers and the 5003rd Airfield Construction Squadron of the RAF combined their efforts to complete the airstrip on schedule.

Although temporarily used by No 122 Sqn in September 1943 because the latter's own ALG at Kingsnorth, Ashford, was being repaired, Brenzett did not come fully into use until July 1944 and the hectic period of the flying bombs. However, by September 1944, the defensive V1 patrols flown by the three squadrons at Brenzett came to an end. For the Mustangs of 133 Wing, the brief but eventful time at the ALG, described in this book, was over, and they moved to Andrews Field, their new home in Essex. Relative peace returned to the fields used by the squadrons, and the villagers of Ivychurch and Brenzett slowly recovered from the friendly invasion to resume their quiet existence.

Today, there is very little to show that there was an ALG close to Brenzett and Ivychurch. Gone are the blister hangars that bore witness to the events of that summer over 50 years ago. Only the Brenzett Aeronautical Museum will continue to be a living memorial to the pilots and ground crews of the squadrons which served on Romney Marsh in 1943 and 1944. Let us hope that we, as a nation, will never forget.

Living accommodation meant tents for pilots and airmen at Brenzett. Note the folding canvas washing facilities in the background. The officer playing with the Alsation dogs is Sqn Ldr S Skalski, who was Wing Leader of 133 Wing for a short period. (Polish Institute).

Chapter One

The Advanced Landing Grounds of Romney Marsh

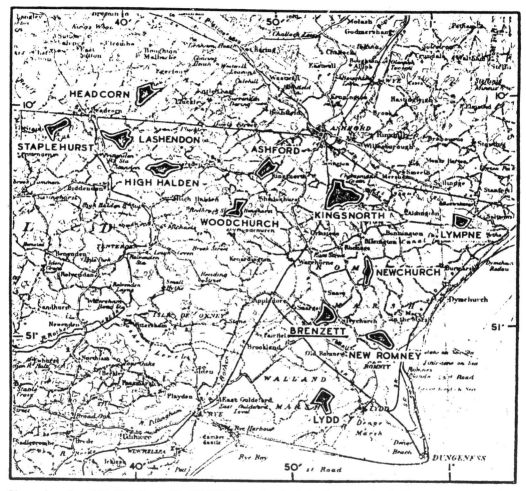

Situated at Lat 51° 1'N, Long 0° 51' 30" E, and only 9 ft above sea level, Brenzett was one of 12 Advanced Landing Grounds located in Kent, SE of London, during 1943-44. RAF Lympne was the nearest permanent airfield to the ALGs on Romney Marsh, but all the bases held strategic importance due to their close proximity to the Continent. (RAF Museum, Hendon).

SUCH famous wartime airfields as Manston, Biggin Hill, Hawkinge and Lympne easily come to mind when the events of the last war are written and discussed. Their importance as part of Kent's aviation heritage is undeniable. Not so well known is the story of 12 temporary airfields, Advanced Landing Grounds, constructed in Kent during 1942-43, and to enjoy a brief, but historically important, existence.

Most new airfields constructed during the RAF's pre-war expansion were located in East Anglia, as the threat of war with Germany increased. In 1940, when France was defeated,

Pilots of No 245 Sqn, 121 Wing, pictured at Lydd (Midley) ALG in the summer of 1943, following their move from Selsey. They flew the Hawker Typhoon and had experienced numerous engine failures at the beginning of the year, but under Sqn Ldr S Hordern, the squadron had persevered with the type and, by the time they reached Lydd, they were conducting coastal patrols and offensive operations over Europe.

the *Luftwaffe* strengthened its bases in the north, and airfields in the Home Counties became particularly vulnerable. So it was that in preparation for the invasion of the continent, Advanced Landing Grounds were constructed in Kent, Sussex and Hampshire. Surveys of suitable locations were undertaken, and many sites were considered. In 1942, those chosen in Kent were Brenzett, New Romney (Honeychild), Lydd (Midley), Newchurch, Ashford (Great Chart), Ashford (Kingsnorth), Woodchurch, High Halden, Headcorn (Egerton), Headcorn (Lashenden), Staplehurst and Swingfield (Folkestone).

These airfields were to be completed by March 1943, and the Royal Engineers Construction Group, together with RAF Airfield Construction Units and the American Engineer Aviation Battalions, would prepare and construct the ALGs. The airfields would be defended by the RAF Regiment and AA units in the area. The ALGs would be used not just by the RAF and Commonwealth squadrons, but would later welcome Fighter Groups of the US 9th Air Force, whilst, from Swingfield, units of the Fleet Air Arm would co-operate with Coastal Command.

Layouts were standardised in having two mesh metal track runways, approximately at right angles to each other, one 1,600 yds and the other 1,400 yds in length, 50 yds wide, with a 50 yd strip cleared either side of the runways. Concrete hardstandings were to be provided for each pair of aircraft. The ALGs would have to accommodate 100 officers and 2,000 other ranks. Any suitable buildings were requisitioned, but for the most part the airmen would have to share tented accommodation.

Of the 12 sites in Kent, four were located close to each other on Romney Marsh at New Romney, Newchurch, Lydd (Midley) and Brenzett. Of these, **New Romney** (Honeychild) was chosen in 1942 in preference to a coastal site at Dymchurch. It was located between St Mary's-in-the-Marsh and the New Sewer, a term used for the marsh drainage channels. One of the problems was the arrangement of streams which crossed the site, solved by drainage and infill. Honeychild Manor would be used for some accommodation, as well as cottages and huts used by an Army Searchlight Battery. This ALG was used to train recently formed mobile squadrons; mobility was essential as these units would need to be able to strike camp and move quickly once the invasion was in progress.

On July 2, 1943, No 124 Wing, comprising Nos 181, 182 and 247 Sqns, arrived from an ALG at Appledram in Sussex. Flying Typhoons, these squadrons operated anti-

The Poles arrive at Brenzett. Airmen unload tents shortly after arrival at the ALG. Accommodation at the flat expanse of pasture was spartan, and most aircrew were to live in tents during their time at Brenzett. (J Polak).

shipping patrols; No 247 would 'soften up' the target and the other two squadrons would deliver their 500 lb (227 kg) bombs with devastating effect. In August 1943, 247 Sqn was involved in preventing 'Hit and Run' raids by the *Luftwaffe* on south-coast towns, while their fellow squadrons carried out similar raids, termed *Rhubarbs*, over the continent, some at night. By October, the weather created such poor conditions at New Romney that 124 Wing moved to Merston, a satellite of Tangmere in West Sussex. The ALG at New Romney became a reserve airstrip for the invasion, and in 1945 the land was handed back to its original owners.

There have been numerous connections with aviation at **Lydd**, the earliest being in 1886 when the Royal Engineers arrived to conduct artillery observation from balloons. Throughout the First World War, units of the Royal Flying Corps flew Artillery Co-operation flights. This early site was located between the B2076 and Dering Farm.

During 1940, a Decoy Airfield was constructed at Midley, two miles north-west of

Lydd. In 1942, the site was selected for construction as an ALG, and was considered an excellent location by the Aerodrome Board, although the area had poor access by road. In 1943, it became operational as a training site for Mobile Fighter Units. The ALG was located at Newland, Upper Agney and Scotts Marsh Farms, but because of objections by the War Agricultural Emergency Committee the site avoided farmhouses and Midley Cottages. As at New Romney, the ALG required drainage and infill before Summerfeld Tracking was laid for its runways. In June 1943, 121 Wing, comprising Nos 174, 175 and 245 Sqns, arrived from ALGs in Sussex. Flying Typhoons, they trained hard. Both Nos 174 and 175 Sqns flew fighter-bomber operations, and No 245 Sqn started with Army Support training, later acting as fighter cover for the other two squadrons on bombing missions.

Squadrons based at Lydd and New Romney took part in Operation *Starkey* during September 1943. On September 15, the ALG was attacked, but with little effect on operations. The ALG's steel mesh tracking suffered

Below: Before moving to the Continent, No 3 Sqn operated Hawker Tempest Vs on anti-flying-bomb patrols from Newchurch as part of 150 Wing. Here, D-Day-striped JF-G receives attention from the ground crew, refuelling from a Bedford QL bowser, rearming and topping up the oil for another mission. Note the blis-ter hangar on the other side of the airfield.

4

under the weight of aircraft taking off and landing, however, and the Wing moved to its new home at Westhampnett (Goodwood), West Sussex, to avoid becoming bogged down at Midley in the coming winter. Lydd continued as a Reserve ALG until it was returned to agricultural use in 1945.

The Advanced Landing Ground at **Newchurch** was constructed on land west of the village between roads connecting Oak Farm and Brookes Farm, missing Wills Farmhouse to the west. Brookes Farm and the Rectory were considered ideal accommodation, the latter being used also for military transport parking, with a dispersal area on the farm.

On July 2, 1943, 125 Wing arrived, comprising Nos 19 and 132 Sqns, which had been previously based at Bognor and Gravesend. These units flew bomber escort missions for the United States Army Air Force, operating from airfields in East Anglia. As at most ALGs, personnel lived in tents, but in July, Orchard House, Bilsington, was also used for accommodation. The two squadrons flew Spitfire VBs, the duties of No 19 Sqn being taken over by No 602 (Glasgow) Sqn in August. They were later joined by No 184 Sqn flying Hurricanes. Their role was that of escort to bomber and fighter

sweeps. After being re-equipped with Spitfire Mk IXs, the Wing moved to Detling, near Maidstone, in October 1943. Then, in April 1944, the ALG was reopened after it had been improved by extending the taxiways and erecting additional blister hangars. No 150 Wing, with Nos 3, 486 (NZ) and 56 Sqns, arrived at Newchurch. Although the Wing was eventually to fly the new Hawker Tempest, only No 3 Sqn was so equipped; in May, No 486 Sqn re-equipped, while No 56 Sqn continued to operate with Spitfire Mk IXs and Typhoons.

The three squadrons at Newchurch immediately began shipping recces, operating in pairs, also attacking transport and airfields. Although ready to tackle the *Luftwaffe*, the Wing was held back to act as air cover over the Invasion on June 6, 1944. Two days later, aircraft of Nos 3 and 486 Sqns shot down four Bf 109s without any loss. On June 13, the Wing was transferred to Air Defence of Great Britain to combat the threat posed by the V1 flying-bombs, which opened a new era of the war and involved squadrons on many airfields. Among them, naturally, were the ALGs in Kent, where 133 Wing, 84 Group, was destined to arrive at Brenzett – with which the remainder of this book is concerned.

Just down the road from Brenzett was the ALG of New Romney and, in July 1943, No 181 Sqn, 124 Wing, was flying Hawker Typhoons from this bleak airfield. Aircraft were coded EL and, commanded by Sqn Ldr Dennis Crowley-Milling, DFC, flew bombing attacks and Rhubarbs across the Channel.

In summer 1942, early North American Mustangs began operations with the RAF. These were Allison-engined Mk 1 aircraft which did not have the performance for high-altitude work, so they were assigned to Army Co-operation Command for low-level photography. No 2 Sqn at Sawbridgeworth was one of half-a-dozen units equipped with the type, and AL995 XV-S served with this squadron and others to survive the war. The camera was housed behind the pilot's position, seen better in the view on page 8.

Chapter 2
Mustang – A brief history

A development Mustang was AL975/G, which was used by Rolls-Royce to fly the higher-powered Merlin 61, seen here, and later the Merlin 65.

THE distinction of being the first single-engined fighter based in Great Britain to penetrate into Germany belongs to the Mustang, and was earned on October 21, 1942, when a number of aircraft of this type attacked targets on the Dortmund-Ems canal, a mission which involved a return flight of 600-700 miles.

The Mustang was a war-baby with an interesting history. It was designed and built to British requirements following a visit by the British Purchasing Commission in April 1940. North American Aviation Inc, of Inglewood, California, was asked to build under sub-contract the single-seat P-40 fighter which was already in production at Curtiss Aircraft. North American countered that request by offering to design and build a completely new fighter incorporating all the latest developments in aircraft design. This proposal was accepted on condition that North American agreed to a time limit of 120 days for the construction of a prototype built round a liquid-cooled engine and embodying certain specified armament and equipment.

Within 100 days, the North American team, under the leadership of Edgar Schmued, the chief design engineer, designed, built and flew

the N.A.73 Mustang, a truly remarkable achievement. Passing all tests satisfactorily, the Mustang was put into production before the end of 1940. The US Army took delivery of two of the prototypes under the designation XP-51 for experimental test at Wright Field, Dayton, Ohio.

The Mustang I was fitted with the Allison V-1710-F3R engine, rated at 1,150 hp at 11,700 ft, and had an armament of four 0.50 in and four 0.30 in machine-guns. Two of the 50 cal guns were mounted in the fuselage, one on each side of the engine crankcase and synchronised to fire through the airscrew, but all the other guns were in the wings. The Mustang I made its first flight in the British Isles in November 1941, and it went into operational use in July 1942.

Although designed as a fighter, the Mustang's powerplant was unsuitable for operation at the heights at which combat was taking place in the skies over Europe. It was therefore re-mustered as a reconnaissance fighter and assigned to Army Co-operation Command. With this Command, the Mustang, equipped with a camera, was used for dual-purpose low-altitude sweeps over enemy-occupied territory, attacking all manner of targets and collecting valuable information, both visual and photographic, for the Allies. The oblique camera for low reconnaissance was installed behind the pilot in place of the port backward-vision panel.

In the meantime, development was proceeding with a view to improving the aircraft's tactical qualities. The Mustang IA appeared with a new Allison engine rated at 1,125 hp at 15,000 ft, and an armament of four 20 mm cannon. This was followed by the Mustang II (P-51A) with an armament of four 0.50 in machine-guns, all in the wings.

It was realised, however, that the Mustang possessed aerodynamic qualities which could be better exploited if a more suitable powerplant could be installed. Several examples were, therefore, fitted with the Merlin engine, the actual conversion being undertaken in England by Rolls-Royce Ltd. Flying trials of the re-engined Mustang confirmed all expectations.

With the Merlin engine being built in the United States by Packard immediate steps were taken by North America to redesign the Mustang to take the new powerplant. The version of the Merlin then in production by Packard was the Mk XX or V-1650-1 but progress was being made in the design and tooling-up for the Packard development of the Merlin 61, known as the V-1650-3, incorporating the Rolls-Royce two-speed two-stage supercharger.

In the meantime, various changes were made in the Allison-powered Mustang to enhance its function as a low-level fighter-bomber so as to maintain production until the new Merlin engine could be introduced onto the production line. Dive-brakes and racks for two 500 lb bombs were fitted to the wings, and thus was evolved the A-36 Invader, which went into action over Sicily and Italy and earned special credit from Lt Gen Carl Spaatz, Commanding the North African Air Forces, for its work in bombing and shooting up tanks, troop concentrations and shipping. The A-36, purely an interim production machine, was the first version of the Mustang, albeit with another name, to be used operationally by the US Army Air Forces. One A-36 was supplied to the RAF for test, but it was never adopted for service by the British forces.

The new Mustang with the Packard V-1650-3 Merlin engine replaced both the Allison-powered P-51 and A-36. It incorporated the best features of both types and, as the Polish-operated squadrons found out, was an outstanding fighter.

A Canadian pilot with the RAF, setting out on an armed reconnaissance flight over northern France, peers out from the cockpit. Behind him is the F.24 camera, which took pictures obliquely between the wing trailing edge and the tailplane. Above the cockpit is a rearview mirror, and behind is the radio mast.

Chapter Three
Brenzett Gets Into Its Stride

TWO Polish-manned squadrons, No 315 (*Deblinski*) and No 306 (*Torunski*), arrived with North American Mustang IIIs from Ford on July 9, 1944, and were shortly joined at Brenzett by No 129 (*Mysore*) Sqn, RAF. These three squadrons had been transferred from the 2nd Tactical Air Force, to form 133 Wing in 84 Group, Air Defence of Great Britain (ADGB). By April 1944, the RAF had taken charge of sufficient numbers of Mustang IIIs to establish another home-based Wing.

The Merlin-powered North American P-51 Mustang was very popular with pilots of the newly-equipped squadrons, which had previously been flying Spitfire VBs and IXs. It was an easy aircraft to fly, and the wide-track undercarriage improved landing, an advantage much needed on the Romney Marsh airstrips. The new enlarged cockpit canopy, or Malcolm hood, gave the pilot improved vision, an advantage in any fighter aircraft.

Also much appreciated was the simple addition of a 'relief tube', perhaps best described by one of the pilots: 'We were highly chuffed because the Mustang was the first kite most of us had flown in which we were able to have a pee!'

Air Chief Marshal Sir Roderick Hill, Commander ADGB, had ordered that aircraft which were to be used exclusively against the V1s should be stripped of their armour and all unnecessary external fittings. The Mustang III was a little slower than the Tempest and at 2,000 ft in level flight, could barely catch up with the V1, even though the aircraft engine had been boosted to achieve a speed of 395 mph.

Many of the V1s crossed the English coast between Cuckmere and St Margaret's Bay. The distance from these locations to the edge of the gun belt was 30 miles, and this the V1 reached in five minutes; the pilots of 133 Wing had little time to reach their target and intercept it. Pilots were at great risk, as they needed to get as close as possible to the V1, which presented such a small target. This meant that the attacking aircraft could be destroyed if the V1's 2,000-lb warhead exploded. A Polish Engineering Officer recalls that 'if the engine of the Mustang, which was fitted with a Rolls-Royce Merlin, was boosted, it could suffer damage after only five minutes.'

The North American Mustang III was one of the outstanding fighter aircraft of the Second World War. This example, FB108, carries dual USAAC/RAF markings before transfer to operational service, joining No 129 Sqn in August 1943, when the type replaced Spitfire IXs. Flown by Flt Lt George Pyle, FB108 crashed in Normandy on June 10, 1944. (MAP).

In late June it was learned that a Spitfire pilot threw a V1 on its back by tipping it with its wing, so that the V1 fell, out of control to explode harmlessly in open country. This tactic was soon being tried by pilots in many other squadrons, the manoeuvre later being improved when pilots would place the wingtip of their aircraft just above or below the wing of the V1, which would destroy its lift and, there-fore, its flight. The pilots at Brenzett talked end-lessly about the tactics of destroying the bombs. The Poles would not attack 'until they could see the red-hot ring of the engine's exhaust nozzle'.

On July 9 and 10, anti-aircraft guns were being relocated to the coast from around London. They were given 10,000 yds range out to sea and 5,000 yds inland, up to 6,000 ft.

Layout of Brenzett in 1945, showing the two runways and the parking bays located off the adjacent taxi-ways. There appears to be four blister hangars on site for maintenance work on the Mustangs. (A E Wright).

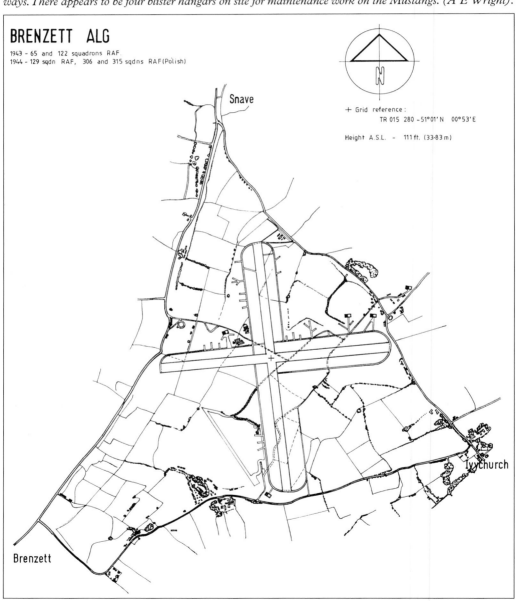

BRENZETT ALG

1943 - 65 and 122 squadrons RAF
1944 - 129 sqdn RAF, 306 and 315 sqdns RAF(Polish)

Snave

+ Grid reference :
TR 015 280 – 51°01'N 00°53'E

Height A.S.L. – 111 ft. (33·83 m)

Iychurch

Brenzett

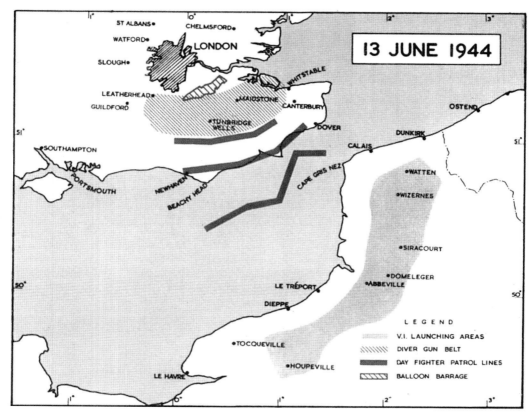

Map showing the defences deployed against the V1 flying-bomb campaign as at June 13, 1944. Despite this 'defence in depth', these 400+ mph weapons still managed to get through to cause extensive damage around the capital.

Balloon units were located some miles out from around the London area, leaving a belt in which the fighters could operate between the guns and the balloons. The first V1 to be destroyed by 133 Wing fell to Flt Sgt Jankowski of No 315 Sqn, on July 11. The following day, P/O Zbrosek shot down three. Both fliers were later noted for perfecting the method of tipping the V1s over, using the Mustang's wingtip (this procedure is described more fully later). On July 22, Flt Lt Stembrowicz shot down his first 'Witch', a term used by the Poles for V1s, when he fired three short bursts at a range of 200 yds down to 100 yds; the V1 crashed just north of Dymchurch, close to the Military Canal.

F/O Holmes was a pilot on No 129 Sqn and recalls with clarity his experiences with the Wing. 'Our role was to fly two-hour patrols along the French coast between Calais and Le Touquet, an activity a lot less exciting than sitting in one's tent at Brenzett, which was partly within the inland AA zone. It rained shrapnel

day and night for several hours at a time, as well as assorted bits of V1 wreckage. I sometimes took a room at the County Hotel in Ashford to catch up on my sleep.

'Our duty roster was that each flight would cover from noon to noon, with the other flight resting, but not leaving the area. The Spitfire and Tempest squadrons (from other ALGs) covered the area between the balloons and the coastal gun zone, flying patrols of one hour or, in the case of the Tempest, 45 minutes. The guns were using proximity fuses for the first time and we gave them the credit for being, at last, almost as good as the German flak – but actually they were remarkably accurate, so much so that the Germans began to hold the 'Doodlebugs' back until they could release about 40 at once and hope to saturate our defences. This made things very dull for the fighters most of the time, except that it gave the Mustangs the best of both worlds. We were still mainly flying the French coast patrols, but in addition we had two aircraft per squadron at

Mustang Emergency!

On May 24, 1944, just two weeks before D-Day, Flt Lt T B Winslow and F/O A D Fraser, of No 268 Sqn based at Gatwick, were briefed to undertake a recce of RDF stations at Neufchatel. Flying Mustang 1As FD497 and 552 respectively, they crossed south of Boulogne and made a diving turn onto the target, both making a perfect approach. Flak was fairly heavy. Fraser saw No 1 pull up in a half roll at 500 ft, streaming smoke. He pulled out on the deck and climbed away, still smoking. The section was pursued out to sea by 20 mm flak. It was not until the section was safely out to sea that Fraser observed that the cockpit hood and flying helmet of his No 1 was missing. Over Brenzett, No 1 decided to land, but was unable to lower the undercarriage. He made a belly landing after two approaches, and was seen to climb from the aircraft. No 2 landed at Gatwick. Subsequently, after emergency treatment, Winslow was flown to base in the Auster and was at once taken to hospital with burns to his face and wrists. He received visitors in the evening and was able to describe how his aircraft had been damaged. Having been hit, flames filled the cockpit. He jettisoned the hood at once and simultaneously lost his helmet. Regaining control, with a burned face and one eye either completely or partially u/s, he reached England and, on seeing an airfield, at once put down the damaged aircraft. From this report, it is clear that Flt Lt Winslow's actions were in every way courageous, and the helpful contact of his escort, exemplary. The lower picture shows US troops, who witnessed the wheels-up landing, inspecting Winslow's aircraft after the incident. (W Smith).

Members of No 129 Sqn pose for a souvenir photo. In the cockpit is 'Stiff' Moreland, with rigger and fitter Jack Lamb and Fred Chapman in the foreground. Note the bulged Malcolm hood which was a great improvement over the basic factory-fitted type, giving much greater visibility. (R. Chapman).

cockpit readiness, at the end of the runways, to help cope with the new saturation tactic.

'When a horde of V1s was detected, the Mustangs on the coast got first crack at them (with very good assistance from our radar stations in II Group), but had to break off pursuit before the guns got our image in their scopes (the guns often picked up our credits for V1s destroyed close to their seaward limit also!).

'All the aircraft at cockpit readiness were scrambled by the firing of a Very light cluster from mid-field. It was an exciting spectacle. Pairs of aircraft came from opposite ends of the same runway, with another pair on the short cross runway. It looked alarming until you knew that the pilots followed rules about which way they would turn before they reached the runway intersection. As we got airborne, we were given sectors to cover, supplemental to the activities of the Spitfires and Tempests, and with the approach of the 'doodlebugs' marked

by the flak, few of them got by except in cloudy weather. It was Battle of Britain all over again! After dark, it was different; night-flying was left in the hands of the Mosquitos and a group of intrepid night-flying Tempest pilots from Boscombe Down Experimental Armament Group.

'We flew our last V1 patrol on September 1, 1944. Tommy Hetherington and I spotted one east of Calais, lost it in cloud for a moment, and then found ourselves ahead of it, and so well placed that it was rolled over by Hetherington's slipstream and forced to dive into the sea.

'It was not unusual for the pilots to wake up in the morning to find that the tent canvas had been torn by fragments of artillery shrapnel. As a precaution, some of them slept with their helmets on!

'Some V1s were attacked at night, but the airstrip at Brenzett was not suitable for night landings and aircraft had to divert to the nearby ALG at Newchurch.

'On return to HQFC, when I reported to my boss, Gp Cpt Bajau, I must have sounded enthusiastic about flying Mustangs, as I found myself posted soon after to 133 Wing, to take over 306 Sqn, my old parent unit.

'On arrival at Brenzett on September 25, I found the situation much changed. There were no more flying-bombs to chase; the advancing Allied forces had taken care of that, having overrun the V1 launching sites. The Wing had already reverted to its original task of high-altitude bomber escorts over Germany. Therefore, the next day I took No 306 Sqn on one of these bomber escorts over the Ruhr, followed by two similar operations on September 30. Between October 2-7, we flew another four sorties, each one of three to four-and-a-half hour duration. The last one was the longest and most spectacular.

'On that occasion (Ramrod 1316), we escorted four Lancasters of Bomber Command to Kembs Dam, across the Rhine, near Mulhouse. Each of the bombers had a specially modified bomb-bay to accommodate one 12,000 lb bomb. They attacked the dam in two waves, first high for earthquake effect, followed by a low one for precision with a delayed action. We were not allowed below 5,000 ft as we would have been caught in the blast. When the first bombs went off, a column of water was flung 1,000 ft into the air; the dam was seen to crack and water began to pour through a break in the western end of the dam. The raid was a great success as it robbed the Germans of the chance to flood the area at a time when the Allied troops were crossing the river. Nevertheless, we paid the price for it; one

Lancaster was shot down by German anti-aircraft fire.

'Although we were a part of the 2nd Tactical Air Force, destined to follow the invading forces to the continent, it was realised that the Mustang's operational long range made it unnecessary for them to move on to the continent. For this reason, it was decided to move our Wing to a base within 11 Group ADGB with concrete runways and other refinements. The station chosen was Andrews Field, near

would open fire. It had been reported that a Spitfire pilot had thrown a V1 on its back by tipping its wing so that it fell out of control. This method was soon tried by pilots from Brenzett and elsewhere. The pilot would position his aircraft's wing either just above or, more often, below, that of the V1, to destroy its lift. However, the danger was that the bomb's wing could swing back with such force that it could damage the wing of the aircraft.

'A strange incident occurred when Flt Lt

A rare photograph of No 129 (Mysore) Sqn at Brenzett in 1944. Back row (l-r): Flt Sgt Guest, W/O Redhead (Red), Flt Lt Osborne (Sammy), W/O Hetherington (Hether), F/O Denny Parker, F/O Jim Hartley, W/O Thomas (Tommy), Cpl Hodgson (Hodge), W/O Foster (Joe), F/O Edwards (Eddie). Middle row (l-r): F/O Thompson (Tommy), Flt Sgt Lane (Chiefy), F/O Holmes (Freddie), F/O Wood (Chippy), Flt Lt Conroy (Guns), F/O Daks Eburne, F/O Nicholson (Nicky), F/O Davies (Dave). Front row (l-r): Flt Lt Mason (Doc), Flt Lt Bassett (Bash), F/O Dickson (Dicky), Flt Lt Ruchwaldy DFM, Sqn Ldr P D Thompson DFC, Flt Lt Leigh (Joe) DFM, Flt Lt Strachen (Storkey), Flt Lt Green (Jerry), F/O Madge (Adjutant) and, not to be forgotten, the mascot, 'JB' (Janny Bush), an Alsation. Not present is squadron member George Pyle, who crashed in Normandy on June 10 on the wrong side of the lines. It took him nine weeks to reach the Allied lines and eventually rejoined 129 at the end of September, having missed the V1 period. The squadron moved to Andrews Field, Essex, the following month.

Braintree, Essex, which had just been vacated by some American units.'

'Shooting down flying-bombs proved to be extremely dangerous, because of the risk of them exploding in the path of the aircraft. Some several hundred rounds were usually expended to bring down one of these small, fast targets, and often, when ammunition was spent, pilots would resort to a fast, close dive into the path of the missile to upset its course through the turbulence created. Another tactic adopted by many pilots was to position the Mustang above, and in front of, the target, and then, as the V1 flew underneath, the pilot

Polak, returning alone with empty machine guns after a heavy engagement with a superior enemy force, became aware of a Bf 109 closing in on him, but not coming in behind him. It flew alongside, wingtip to wingtip, and remained with him until halfway across the Channel; then, with a wave, they parted company to fight another day. Flt Lt Polak assumed that the '109 was also without ammunition.

'An unfortunate episode occurred when two Polish pilots, Flt Sgt Lewicki and Sgt Walasek of No 315 Sqn, were on patrol. They were directed inland, which was unusual. That day, the Beachcraft (apparently another codename for a V1), seemed to be flying over in droves; an interval followed, then in came the next wave. The pilots were told that a V1 had crossed the coast and had evaded the guns and was close to their position. Suddenly, they spotted their quarry and Walasek closed in. He got into the line of flight of the bomb in preparation for a kill. Suddenly a Tempest appeared high above and, taking no notice of the two Mustangs, dived at the V1 at terrific speed. It got in front of Sgt Walasek, who had to take swift evasive action. Two other Tempests appeared; the first hardly had a chance to fire when he was bounced by an American P-47 Thunderbolt which took up the chase, positioning himself on the Tempest's tail. The pilot opened fire through the other aircraft in front of him. Flt Sgt Lewicki peeled away. Sgt Walasek had been hit and he made for Brenzett. Two of the Tempests were also hit, but made it back to base at Newchurch; the third climbed vertically, escaping the Thunderbolt's fire. The V1 continued on its way untouched.

'The CO of No 316 Sqn, based at Friston, Sussex, visited Brenzett to see Sqn Ldr Eugeniusz Horbaczewski VM, KW, DFC and Bar, who was the CO of No 315 Sqn. After a pleasant chat, Horbaczewski strolled off to change his uniform. As he did so, guns began to roar and a familiar shape, a V1, was seen heading towards the airfield at low altitude. On reaching the perimeter of the ALG it dived as if hit by gunfire. The visitor looked around for shelter; there was none, so he threw himself flat on the ground. Meanwhile, the bomb started to climb to the west. Sqn Ldr Bohdan Arct picked himself up, and nearby mechanics dusted themselves down and returned to their duties. Much to everyone's surprise, the V1 turned east towards France, from where it had come. Then, as if it had had a change of mind, it turned to circle the astonished airmen. Yet again, the persistent bomb dived towards the airfield, and again pulled up; everyone was relieved to see the intruder head off at last towards London; or so they thought – it turned again, but this time it dropped down behind the distant hills and exploded.'

A pilot of No 129 Sqn, P/O 'Chippy' Woods, remembers that on one occasion a V1 exploded on the airstrip, killing some of the local sheep. As a result, the squadrons feasted rather well for a few days on roast lamb!

Sqn Ldr J Z Zulikowski, of No 315 Sqn, remembers his time at Brenzett as being only a fortnight. 'Prior to my official posting to No 306 Sqn, I visited 133 Wing twice in my new capacity of a Staff Officer at HQFC. On both occasions, I took the opportunity to get familiar with Mustang aircraft and did some local flying. During my second visit, I even had the opportunity to give chase to a V1, which just happened to have crossed the coastline on its way to London. However, as I was inching my approach to his tail, a Tempest dived in front of me and got the bug first, which exploded instantly. As one of the main routes of the flying-bombs was passing over Brenzett, it was a great show to watch our fighters pursuing these intruders without regard to the anti-aircraft guns' shells, which competed successfully with our fighters by using proximity fuses, thus creating a high rate of scoring. During the night, the artillery, being left in the field on their own, was doubling the effort to get the bombs. It was unnerving to find, the following morning, our canvas tents torn by the fragments of artillery shrapnel. No wonder that some wore helmets during their sleep, for protection!

'By this time, Allied troops were in Brussels and Antwerp, but the Germans still held out in Boulogne, Ostend and the Antwerp docks, and kept the Scheldt closed by holding the 'Breskens Pocket'. The 2nd TAF was still operating mainly from the Normandy airfields and was having trouble overcoming supply problems in competition with the armies – British and US.

'Early in August, a series of one-squadron shows was laid on, whereby one of the Brenzett squadrons would take the day off from V1s and help to maintain Allied air superiority over the battle area and from Beauvais to Arnhem. From September 2-16, the Wing flew armed reconnaissance out from the Arnhem/Nijmegen area, and became the long-range fighter escort to Bomber Command Halifaxes and Lancasters flying against targets in the Ruhr. We carried 75 US gallon drop tanks for the first time.

'From September 17-26, we flew anti-flak and fighter cover for the Allied air fleet and parachutists taking part in Operation *Market Garden* at Arnhem, and the follow-up supply drops. On one day we were among the 1,000 Allied fighters covering the area around Grave, while hundreds of Dakotas landed supplies at a hastily-prepared airstrip. There was a lot of cloud about and we later estimated that we had one near-miss a minute! That was a lot of aircraft to crowd into the available airspace. We shot down several German fighters during the period and lost a few ourselves.

'Our losses during the V1 period (omitted above), were four pilots killed, two from No 129 Sqn and one each from Nos 306 and 315 Sqns. One of the snags with the 6,000-ft ceiling for the AA guns was that clouds were often

A Spitfire XIV of No 129 Sqn when it was operating in Norway between June and November 1945. The aircraft is fitted with underwing bomb-racks and, although the engine is running, no figure is visible in the cockpit – no doubt the occupant is busy 'heads-down'. (F Jarvis).

below this height. They gave us a safety lane near Hastings which was not marked in any way and which was too narrow. After the flak shot down one of the Poles when we believed he was in the safety lane (because, they said, the aircraft was flying fast enough to be a V1; well, we had to be or we were wasting a lot of time!), we flew a sort of slalom through the lane, just in case. After September 26, we began daylight escorts with Bomber Command deep inside Germany, which continued until the end of the war.

'On October 7, just after lunch, No 617 Sqn's Lancasters flew above Brenzett's main runway at 50 ft and drew No 129's Mustangs, already idling in position, into the air en route for Kembs, close to the Swiss border at Basle, to attack a dam. They were led by Jimmy Tait, who was taking time off from training for the Tirpitz attack.

'We spent October 9 and 10 moving out of Brenzett to Andrews Field, near Braintree. (Known, until May 21, 1943, as Great Saling, Andrews Field was the first airfield constructed in Britain by the US Pioneer Corps, and was named after the late Lt Gen F M Andrews. It was vacated by the USAAF in September 1944, and quickly became home to some 100 Mustang IIIs in the hands of RAF squadrons No 19, 65, 122, 129, 306, 315 and 316.) We were joined at Andrews Field by Nos 19, 65 and 122 Sqns, which had served with 83 Group

TAF from Normandy to Brussels in the same Mustang IIIs as 122 Wing. Both Wings now came under 12 Group Fighter Command, but lost their 122 and 133 prefixes.

'Gp Capt Nowierski and the HQ Unit was 100% Polish. The Wg Cdr Flying was also Polish, first Wg Cdr S K Skalski and, from about July 15, 1944, Wg Cdr Jan Zumbach (who preferred to be called John).

'But night flying was really hairy at Brenzett. The old gooseneck flares would have been an improvement over the pitiful string of electric bulbs provided there. Our first and last V1 patrols each day took off and landed in the dark, but there had been no night operations until, on September 5, No 129 Sqn was sent over Holland at dusk to confirm their sighting earlier of heavy German traffic just north of Antwerp. Wg Cdr Zumbach went along with us for the ride. Because of a bad crosswind at Brenzett, Sector Control ordered the squadron to land at Newchurch, where there was better lighting and an asphalt runway. Ten aircraft did so and were guided to parking places in the dark by hand-held flashlights, resulting in five of them being steered into a ditch. (The resident squadrons, 56, 3 and 486, wondered how they could get credit for the destruction of five Mustangs . . . !) The other two aircraft, Wg Cdr Zumbach and F/O Holmes, landed at Brenzett. The Wing Commander went through the far fence and destroyed some barrels set as

17

Pilots of No 122 Sqn, pictured at Kingsnorth ALG, where they were based with Nos 65 and 602 Sqns in September 1943. A detachment operated briefly from Brenzett during the period July to October 1943. CO at the time was Sqn Ldr Peter Wickham, DFC. (RAF Museum, Hendon).

perimeter markers (unlit, of course) and I, although terrified, made a decent landing for a change.'

One of the first local residents to see a flying-bomb passing over Brenzett was a young Land Army girl living with her parents on their farm: 'The noise was unlike anything we had heard before. At first we thought it was a plane with engine trouble, but on looking through the window we could see nothing but a black shape with sheets of flame spurting out behind it. We all rushed downstairs and outside, but it was too dark to see much more. The most amazing thing was the reaction of the American soldiers stationed around the area. They let fly with anything that would fire, mostly small weapons, and it was like a firework display.'

In May 1944, the 406th Fighter Group of the US Ninth Air Force, comprising the 512th, 513th and 514th Fighter Squadrons, based at the ALG at Ashford (Great Chart), used Brenzett ALG for operations in preparation for the invasion. The purpose of this training was to prepare the squadrons for rapid movement, which would be essential when the big day came.

Organisation of the move to Brenzett was the principal responsibility of the various sections in the headquarters, which were already carrying the operational load. The personnel of the organisation were divided between air and ground echelon, and each section prepared to operate in two sections on movement. It was conceived that any moves affecting a mobile unit such as the 406th FG would require the air echelon moving out first to the destination to establish the Advanced Landing Ground – in this case Brenzett. In the interim, the flight echelon would be operated by the ground echelon until such time as the squadrons were established.

This procedure was outlined by the American HQ section and on May 23 the practice training move was made to Brenzett, approximately 15 miles from the ALG at Ashford. The first units to arrive were the Operations and Intelligence Sections, plus all the communications equipment; these, operating from vehicles, moved out of Ashford at 0600 hrs. A mission was received, briefed and flown from the regular base by the ground echelon, landing at Brenzett, and shortly after midday they were received by the Air echelon. By 1500 hrs, the ground echelon had moved to Brenzett and was able to operate at full strength. On May 24, a similar operation was carried out, but in reverse, and was handled without any major problem. However, the move highlighted the necessity for travelling as light as possible.

Chapter Four

No 129 (*Mysore*) Squadron

ON July 8, the usual panic ensued as personnel of 133 Wing were told that they were to move from Ford the following day. As seemed to be usual when 133 Wing moved, the weather was down, so that they were unable to fly. Their new home was Brenzett ALG; their mission, to seek and destroy V1s, better known to No 129 Sqn as 'Chuff Boxes'. They were to start operations the next day and, judging by the number of V1s passing over the area, they were going to have a lot of work.

At 1300 hrs the next day, the Wing commenced *Diver* patrols and flew until dusk. Many flying-bombs were seen that day but, despite seven patrols being flown, none was destroyed, and the eager pilots were rather shaken by the speed of Germany's terror weapon. Later in the day, Flt Lt Bassett and Flt Lt Baker managed to destroy one V1, at 1920 hrs, near Hythe.

At 1200 hrs the following day, F/O Holmes destroyed another near Hastings, followed at 2115 hrs by F/O Hartley, when he blew one up in mid-air. Fourteen patrols were recorded that day.

During the following day, 13 patrols were flown by No 129 Sqn, with greater success, as they shot down seven V1s. The first came down at Dungeness, destroyed by P/O Edwards, followed by Flt Lt Kleimeyer, who destroyed one north of Beachy Head. Again, F/O Holmes added to the score by bringing one down at Folkestone. As if to prove a point, Flt Lt Ruchwaldy destroyed two, one at Folkestone, swiftly followed by another at Lympne. Flying north of Hastings, F/O Baker took one out, and the day ended well when W/O Redhead and P/O Bilodeau shared one as it crashed dramatically into the sea some 15 miles off Hastings.

On August 19, three flying-bombs were shot

The men who gave the Spit its firepower. N-NUTS provides the background for a group shot of the armament section of No 129 (Mysore) Sqn, when based at Gardermoen, Norway, in August 1945. (F Jarvis)

down in the course of 14 patrols flown by the squadron. Flt Lt Ruchwaldy destroyed the first, three miles north-west of Hastings. The C/O, Sqn Ldr P D Thompson, destroyed the second south-east of Hastings and Flt Lt Strachen the third, three miles south-east of Tunbridge Wells.

During the afternoon of July 22, nine Diver Patrols were flown, ten bombs being destroyed; Sgt Sandover got the first, Flt Sgt Jeal the second, near Ashford, and F/O Osborne and F/O Parker shared one, which also crashed in the area of Ashford. F/O Osborne later destroyed another a mile north of Ashford; W/O Redhead caught one at Hythe and chased it as far as Maidstone, where it was seen heading away from the town, but was not seen to crash owing to dense cloud. Flt Lt Ruchwaldy destroyed anther at 2015 hrs and F/O Holmes and F/O Parker shared two – the first near Appledore and the second near Ashford; Flt Lt Osborne got another one two miles south-east of Tonbridge. The last of the day was destroyed by Flt

A dramatic action shot of a V1 diving to the ground near the tented area at Brenzett! In fact, this was a wooden model suspended to produce a hoax picture – remembered clearly by a member of No 6129 Service Echelon attached to No 129 Sqn. (F Jarvis).

Early in August 1944, a V1 was shot down by a pilot of 129 Sqn, which crashed and exploded in a field one mile NW of the airstrip. A group of pilots jumped in the squadron truck and sped to the site. Unfortunately, the bomb landed among some sheep, killing many of them. The farmer arrived about the same time as the pilots; he was furious! He wanted to know why they didn't 'drop the bloody things into empty fields rather than in the midst of his sheep!' The assembled group expressed their dismay at the damage caused and tried to explain that it was often not possible to place the bloody things with such precision. After a while he calmed down, but the pilots felt he was more angry with them than the Germans! As they left the scene, they retrieved a wing from the V1, about the only piece of any size still intact, and took it back to the Squadron dispersal tent were it was proudly displayed. F/O Mike Humphries painted the squadron's crest on the trophy, adding a figure of a V1 for every one shot down by them. By September 25, 1944, the tally had reached 56. Unfortunately, despite enquiries, the wing has since disappeared, although it was taken with 129 Sqn to Andrews Field, their next base, early in October 1944, where this interesting photograph was taken by F/O Fred Holmes.

Lt Bassett, four miles south-east of Ashford. A successful day for all.

The following day, 14 patrols were flown. F/O Dickson shared a V1 with a Spitfire six miles south of Maidstone. F/O Parker destroyed two, the first at Tenterden, shared with a Spitfire, while the second was seen to crash six miles north-west of Ashford. During this combat, an aircraft was seen firing behind F/O Parker, an unpleasant experience.

On August 3, flying conditions were ideal, with a 10/10 layer of thin cloud at about 1,500 ft; any flak or V1s would be silhouetted against the sky. Pilots of 'A' Flight claimed eight, Sqn Ldr Strachan two, Flt Lt Kleimeyer two-and-a-half, Flt Lt Green one-and-a-half, and F/O Hartley and F/O Lunn one each. F/O Lunn was momentarily surprised when a *Diver* blew up in the air and threw his Mustang on its back. Fortunately, the aircraft was only slightly damaged and he was able to return to Brenzett, landing without incident.

Four flying-bombs were added to the squadron score on August 5, when F/Os Twomey, Humphries, Holmes and P/O Edwards claimed one each. The beginning of August was hot, and pilots of 'A' Flight took

advantage of this by spending the afternoon swimming in the sea off Dungeness.

The following afternoon, W/O Redhead intercepted and destroyed a V1 just north of the airfield. This was quite entertaining as members of 133 Wing had a grandstand view.

About this time, many of the pilots complained of the number of aircraft competing with each other to shoot down a single bomb, a situation which proved irritating as the target had sometimes been allotted to them by control. There were two quite busy hours early on in the morning of August 7, when the V1s came over thick and fast. W/O Hartley added a couple to his score, which meant he kept his position as the squadron's 'top gun', with six. P/O Edwards was hard on his heels, but gave the other pilots a fright when, after damaging a V1 which had also been hit by flak, he dived towards the dispersal area, finally forced landing in a field and killing several sheep.

By August 17, 133 Wing was operating *Ranger* patrols twice a week, which pleased the pilots of No 129 Sqn. On that day, aircraft were despatched on patrol, but the weather was very poor and nothing was seen. In the Paris, Lille

The Signals Section of No 6129 Service Echelon in front of Mustang DV-B. Left to right: Ralph Hutchinson, Stan Collett, Vic Marshall, Harry Watkins, Tom Fox and Dougie Body. (R Huntsman).

and Brussels area, there was a chance of meeting the new German jet aircraft.

Another *Ranger* of eight aircraft was flown on the following afternoon to the Beauvais-Soissons and Cambrai areas, but nothing was seen. This was to be expected after No 315 Sqn's magnificent effort earlier that day, when they encountered 24 Fw 190s taking off from Beauvais and had shot down 16. In a separate sortie, Flt Lt Ruchwaldy destroyed a V1 with his slipstream off Boulogne.

The following day, August 19, turned out to be a successful one: F/O Hartley boosted his score when he destroyed one *Diver* off

destruction. F/O Twomey destroyed another on the French coast at Cap Gris Nez.

Sea patrols continued: on August 29, the squadron destroyed another six and claimed two 'halves'. F/O Hartley opened the scoring just before midday when he shot one down ten miles south of Folkestone; F/O Osborne and F/O Wood got one each, and F/O Bassett shared another with the flak. Finally, Flt Lt Ruchwaldy returned from patrol in the evening and claimed three-and-a-half destroyed; the first he shot at and observed strikes, but the V1 then entered the gun belt and was destroyed by the flak. Two others he caught in his slipstream

Belts of 0.5 in ammunition being fed into the wing bays of a 129 Sqn Mustang, ready for the next sortie. The wing guns have yet to be taped over, a standard procedure to prevent icing at altitude. After the guns had been fired, the ports produced a distinctive whistling sound, alerting those on the ground that the aircraft had been in action. (Polish Institute).

Boulogne and possibly another, although he did not see it crash. That evening, W/O Redhead and W/O Hetherington scored one each while on patrol over the sea; the latter fired at two but missed and, having used all his ammunition, then made one spin by getting in front of it and upsetting it with his slipstream.

On August 20, P/O Bilodeau was killed when his Mustang, FB395, crashed at Kingsnorth, Ashford: the aircraft spun into the ground after being seen climbing through cloud. P/O Wood destroyed his first *Diver*; although he did not see it hit the ground, Biggin Hill confirmed its

and, finally, as his guns had jammed, he tipped one into the sea with his wing.

By the end of the month, the squadron score stood at 59-and-a-half, 15 of which were still to be confirmed. They had put in 50 claims, pushing their score up into the nineties.

At the beginning of September the rumour spread that the squadron was soon to change its *Diver* patrols for another job. On September 3, after uneventful patrols at dawn, the squadron was warned for an escort job in the afternoon, and many felt that they had seen the last of the 'Doodlebugs'. But it was not to be . . . For the

An American anti-aircraft battery situated close to New Romney at the height of the V1 campaign. Towards the end of the onslaught, 90% of V1s were said to have been destroyed by the defensive gun belt and the squadrons that intercepted them. Tragically, some aircraft were accidentally shot down and pilots killed by anti-aircraft fire. (Kent Messenger).

next few weeks, No 129 Sqn shared its time between patrolling the Dieppe-Cayeux area and the inland patrols between Hastings and Folkestone, the latter being far more fruitful thanks to better controlling from 'Gin-Fizz'. As the British Second Army in France advanced and crossed the Seine and began to menace the launching sites in the Dieppe area, the patrols

A sketch by Mr B Shearing, who served in the Army and made several visits to ALGs in the Romney area. It shows Hawker Tempest JF-E, flown by Flt Sgt M J Rose, which force-landed at Brenzett on June 23, 1944. Whether the spinner was missing from action over France or had been removed after landing is not recorded.

were moved up the French coast to cover Cayeux-Boulogne and, eventually, Boulogne-Calais. This latter period out to sea was fairly productive and, because of the accuracy of the coastal AA, was preferred to the inland patrol. The squadron's final confirmed score at that time was 66 – the top scoring squadron on the Wing. Flt Lt Ruchwaldy was the highest scorer in the squadron with eight, and he reached the headlines in the daily press.

In the afternoon, the squadron was briefed to escort ten Mosquitos bombing Venlo and Volkel airfields in Holland. The rendezvous was not made, but the six aircraft which went to Venlo saw the target being heavily bombed by Halifaxes.

The following day there were no operations: time for the usual low-level missions to the 'County' in Ashford and the 'George' in Rye!

On September 5, the squadron had a fairly successful beat-up during the afternoon in the south of Holland. Two lorries were destroyed near Amersfoort and two damaged at Vianne.

The enemy on its way! A V1 shortly after leaving its launch ramp in northern France. The Argus pulse-jet produced a rhythmic sound and gave the unmanned bomb a speed of more than 400 mph. When the fuel ran out, the engine stopped and the weapon plunged to the ground.

A locomotive and ten tankers were attacked and destroyed between Elst and Nijmegen, in the face of some intense light flak. In addition to this, a very large convoy of MET was seen entering Dorreout and a large vessel was seen beached and on fire by the Dutch island of Thoien. So it was with high hopes that the squadron took off again for another reconnaissance. This was led by Wg Cdr Zumbach in the Nijmegen area at dusk. The light was failing, however, and nothing was seen, and the aircraft had to land at Newchurch ALG as Brenzett did not have night landing facilities.

Not all Doodlebugs, or V1s, exploded when they crashed, as can be seen here. This gave RAF personnel and Bomb Disposal Units the opportunity to inspect the remains. This particular wreckage is in a field on Romney Marsh.

On September 13, 12 aircraft took off to go to Hendon with the Wing, prior to escorting a VIP to Paris. The weather north of London was very hazy, but after a bit of trial and error navigation, the squadron reached Hendon, which was nearly completely 'clamped'. The haze cleared a little, however, and the Wing took off with the three Dakotas carrying the VIP and entourage, escorting them uneventfully to Paris. After beating up Le Bourget in formation, they returned at zero feet over the French countryside, climbing up over the sea to head for home.

In the afternoon, the squadron was on an escort and withdrawal cover for Halifax bombers attacking Osnabruck. There was the usual inaccurate flak and the bombers did the usual good job. One particularly large explosion was seen, causing a great mushroom of black smoke to 8,000 ft; one member of the squadron remarked that he would have liked to pick it up and take it home (it being the height of the mushroom season in the fields around the base!). Otherwise, the trip was uneventful and closed a busy day for the Wing.

Next day, No 129 took on a very interesting job, acting as anti-flak to the great airborne invasion of Holland. They escorted some of the gliders in and then, along the patrol line Zevenbergen-Hertogenbosh, light AA posts and flak towers were strafed and silenced. One ammunition dump was exploded by bombing. Troops crossing the river on a bridge at Feneboon offered a magnificent target. A radar station came in for some attention east of Costerhout. Four Fw 190s were seen west of Hertogenbosh, but could not be caught.

On September 25, the squadron was on a Ramrod escorting Mitchells and Bostons bombing gun positions in the Arnhem area and, for the first time for many months, encountered the *Luftwaffe*. There were an estimated 50+ Fw 190s and Bf 109s in small groups, and two squadrons attacked with more eagerness than skill. F/O Humphries and Flt Lt Howard were both shot down, though both believed safe, and both scored before they were attacked; F/O Humphries destroyed an Fw 190 and Howard damaged a Bf 109. Flt Lt Parker destroyed an Fw 190, though there was some argument as to what type it was; Flt Lt Bassett destroyed a '109 and F/O Dickson shot down an Fw 190.

The squadron acted as escort, the next day, to heavy bombers over the Ruhr. The Halifaxes bombed through 9/10 cloud, but smoke and explosions were seen; there was some inaccurate flak. On the way out, Blue Section (Blue 2 having previously turned back) were detailed to cover a lone bomber which was in trouble and far behind the main stream. It was left trailing behind No 129 and having done its job, the squadron descended through cloud and headed home. However, Blue 4 developed glycol trouble in the cloud and was forced to land in flooded fields just north of Antwerp. At the time, it was not known whether or not this was behind Allied lines, but the pilot later reported that he was safe. Blue 3 then developed identical trouble and had to land south of Dunkirk. The pilot was not injured and was soon picked up by a Jeep, according to F/O Dickson (Blue 1); considerably shaken, he returned to Brenzett without further incident.

On the afternoon of October 7, the Wing acted as escort and anti-flak to a force of 13 Lancasters on a dam-busting raid just north of Basle on the French-Swiss-German frontier. The Lancasters were to bomb in two waves, the first six aircraft at 8,000 ft, and the second wave at zero feet. Acting as top cover to the high force were No 129, while No 315 covered the low force, and No 306 were anti-flak. The rendezvous over Dungeness and the flight out to Besancon went according to plan; the low force then did an orbit and went on with the high force, meeting a little flak on the way to the target. The bombing was fairly accurate, though some were not close; the first bomb scored almost a direct hit. The fun started when the low force went in; the first aircraft came in for some intense flak from positions near the dam, and called for assistance from No 306, which then went in and strafed the flak. The next bomber, however, was badly hit and crashed just after it had gone over the dam. The flak then more or less succumbed to the strafing and several of the low-level force placed their delayed action bombs with accuracy. Remaining over the target until the last bomber had finished its job, No 129 turned towards home, leaving the inspiring view of the Swiss Alps behind.

There were no operations on the following day, and no mention of the previous day's dam-busting raid in the newspapers. Reconnaissance had shown that the dam had been broken and the land downstream had been well flooded. Basle reported that the water level had dropped 14 ft.

On October 10, following two days without operations, the Wing was moved to Andrews Field near Braintree, a change which had been in the air for some time. The airfield there was excellent, with long runways, but the first reconnaissance of the surrounding area was not so promising, and some of the pubs visited were not up to standard!

Chapter Five
No 306 (*Torunski*) Polish Squadron

ON July 9, 1944, this squadron arrived at Brenzett at 2210 hrs, the ground crew having travelled by road from RAF Ford. The following day, Flt Sgt Rudowski, on his first mission, shot down a V1. Fourteen patrols were flown. Flt Lt Siekierski was reposted as Flight Commander 'A' Flight.

Twenty-six patrols were flown on July 11, one V1 being destroyed by Flt Lt Siekierski.

In the afternoon of July 12, Flt Sgt Nowoczyn shot down two and Flt Lt Beyer one V1. A most unfortunate event occurred while one young pilot was on leave at Heston. His wife and daughter were among those killed by a V1; he was injured in the explosion. This came as a great shock for all his comrades at Brenzett.

P/O Bzowski destroyed a V1 on July 15, P/O Wacnik destroyed two, Flt Sgt Nowoczyn and Flt Sgt Zalenski one each on July 16. Seventeen *Diver* patrols were flown on July 17, and no fewer than 32 on July 18, with Flt Lt Siekierski claiming one V1 destroyed. The following day, Flt Sgt Zaworski and Flt Sgt Rudowski shot down three *Divers*, two of them on the same patrol; 26 patrols were flown by the squadron.

On July 20, Flt Lt Potocki was awarded the DFC for gallantry. Whilst chasing a V1, P/O Kawniks' Mustang was hit by 'friendly' anti-aircraft fire.

Following two days of relative peace, No 306 Sqn had their best day on July 22, when nine V1s were destroyed. The first was shot down by Flt Sgt Rudowski, then three were destroyed by Flt Lt Siekierski; P/O Kawnik

Members of 306, 309, 315 and 316 Polish Sqns at a briefing at Andrews Field, the airfield to which 133 Wing moved after leaving Brenzett in October 1944. The word 'Greengrocer', seen on the blackboard, was the callsign for the 21st Base Defence Wing, 2nd Tactical Air Force. The airfield layout on the wall is thought to be Andrews Field. (W Smith).

destroyed two more. Another was shot down by F/O Tronczynski and two by F/O Gierjcz. Perfecting their newly-acquired skill, F/O Tronczynski shot down two on July 23, and

On August 18, 1944, P/O F M Migos of 306 Sqn was killed when his aircraft, FB206, crashed 1.5 miles west of Ham Street. Spitfire NH713 of 130 Sqn entered the formation and collided with P/O Migos and tore off one of the Mustang's wings. The aircraft plunged to earth; its pilot had no chance of survival. He is buried at Brookwood cemetary. (W Smith).

North American Mustang III, FZ149, of No 306 Sqn, plugged into a trolley-acc ready for action. As with most Polish-operated aircraft, this carries a small national marking on the nose. To prevent confusion with German fighters like the Bf 109, Mustangs were given white stripes on the top surfaces of the wing and tailplane in addition to bands around the nose and rear fuselage. Just visible are the remains of D-Day stripes around the fuselage roundel.

P/O Migos and Flt Lt Marschall claimed one each.

Tragedy struck the next day, when W/O Machowiak was killed on a cross-country flight in a communications Auster. The squadron was appalled by the news as he had served with No 306 for a long time. One *Diver* was destroyed by Flt Lt Beyer, and a half was claimed by P/O Kawnik. The squadron's score rose on July 26, when Flt Sgt Zalenski destroyed three V1s, Flt Lt Beywer and Sqn Ldr Niemiec a half each, and Flt Sgt Czezowski claimed one.

The routine of daily patrols intensified. Next day, Flt Sgt Rudowski claimed one-and-a-half, W/O Pomietlarz one, and P/O Smigielski one-and-a-third, V1s. On the following day, 27 patrols were flown but only P/O Smigielski and Flt Sgt Zalenski claimed two destroyed.

July 29 was another day of tragedy. P/O Zygmund took off from Brenzett to carry out a *Diver* patrol in the Hastings area, with Flt Lt Marschall as his No 2. Approaching Hastings, they were fired on by our own anti-aircraft guns about six miles from the coast. P/O Zygmund was hit by flak and killed when his Mustang burst into flames and hit the sea. A court of enquiry was held at RAF Hawkinge. Twenty-six patrols were flown that day and Flt Sgt Zalenski shot down one V1.

On July 30, Flt Sgt Czezowski and Flt Sgt Zalenski together destroyed one V1. The PWR (Polish *Virtuti Militari* – Vth Class) was awarded to the following pilots for their gallantry: Flt Lt Beywer, P/O Potocki and P/O Marschall. On that day, 32 patrols were carried out by No 306 Sqn. Flt Sgt Rudowski closed the score of the squadron's first hectic month on one of its 18 patrols on July 18, by destroying another flying-bomb.

On August 3, the first pilot of No 306 Sqn to have shot down a V1, Flt Sgt Rudowski, added to his score by claiming one-and-a-half destroyed; Flt Sgt Czezowski also shot one down. Between the hours of 0500 and 1300 on August 4, the squadron flew 22 patrols and accounted for four V1s.

On August 5, Flt Lt Smigielski and W/O Nowoczyn destroyed one 'doodlebug' each, and on August 6, three more were destroyed by Flt Lt Siekierski. On the following day, P/O Waznik accounted for two and Flt Sgt Zalenski, one.

The DFC was awarded to F/O Pietrzak on August 14. F/O Lazskiewicz was reported as having been taken prisoner, unharmed, following his disappearance on June 11. The same day, W/O Nowoczyn destroyed a V1.

An unusual event occurred on August 16 when Flt Sgt Rudowski attacked a V1 at the precise moment machine gun fire from a Gloster Meteor, struck his Mustang. Fortunately, he was not injured. The Meteor was most probably one from No 616 (South Yorkshire) Sqn, based at RAF Manston, although it could have been on detachment at High Halden, an ALG near Tenterden.

August 18 proved to be a sad day for 133 Wing at Brenzett, as both No 306 and 315 lost pilots. Sqn Ldr Horbaczewski lost his life over Beauvais, as previously described, and aircraft of No 306 were involved in a tragic accident. The squadron was forming up over Brenzett for a Ranger patrol when a lone Spitfire entered the formation. It struck the starboard wing of Mustang FB206, flown by P/O Migos, which was torn off on impact. The aircraft, with its pilot trapped, spun into the ground one-and-a-half miles west of Ham Street.

On August 23, Flt Lt Klawe claimed half a V1 destroyed, while five days later W/O Pomietlarz and Flt Lt Wisiorek each shot down a V1.

Much to everyone's relief, Flt Sgt Mrozowski, reported missing on June 21, was now reported as having been taken prisoner. During his spell in hospital at RAF Cosford, W/O Krupa was posted to RAF Hawkinge on August 30.

During the first two weeks of September, No 306 Sqn flew many escort duties and patrols, although the V1 campaign was coming to its conclusion and anti-*Diver* patrols were not so frequent.

On September 17, during anti-flak opera-

W/O J Czezowski of No 306 Sqn hugs his pet dog, relieved to be back at Brenzett after an operational sortie. (Polish Institute).

A small, but remarkable, surviving piece of history is the starboard wingtip panel from the Mustang flown by P/O Migos. It is stored at the Tangmere Aviation Museum and clearly shows the US marking under the RAF roundel. The aileron is still attached and the three circular holes originally held identification lights. (Author).

tions, Flt Sgt Dowgalski was hit while flying in the vicinity of Zevenbergen-Hertogenbosch; his aircraft cockpit was shattered and, on return to Brenzett, he was taken to hospital at nearby Willesborough, Ashford.

Returning from RAF Friston, Sussex, after having taken part in Operation *Market Garden*, on September 21, W/O Krupa crashed on take-off. He was slightly injured and admitted to Princess Alice Hospital, Eastbourne, and the next day moved to Queen Victoria Hospital, East Grinstead.

Weather conditions were good on September 25 when 11 pilots of No 306 Sqn took off from Brenzett for *Ramrod 1295*. They were to act as air cover to paratroops in the Arnhem area and met a formation of enemy aircraft over the target area and, in the ensuing battle, F/O Smigielski managed to damage one of the German aircraft. Sqn Ldr Zulikowski reported to Brenzett, having been posted from ADGB, taking over command from Sqn Ldr Niemic; acting ranks of Sqn Ldr were retained in both cases.

The next day, during Operation *Market Garden*, nine aircraft acted as target cover over landing strips at Graves. On the 27th, nine Mustangs of No 306 escorted Halifax bombers on *Ramrod 1297*. Flt Sgt Koloczyk, who was last seen flying about two miles east of North Foreland when the squadron was on its way to the target area, failed to return and was presumed to have become lost in cloud and to have crashed into the sea; he was reported missing. Other pilots returned at 1135 hrs.

Flt Lt Wedzik was hit by flak on September 28 over Emmerich on *Ramrod 1299*, but landed back at Brenzett at 1020 hrs uninjured. Two days later, nine pilots escorted heavy bombers to oil installation targets at Sterkrade on *Ramrod 1302*, landing back at base at 1400 hrs. On October 5, the squadron acted as penetration and withdrawal cover to bombers attacking Wilhelmshaven; Flt Lt Beyer had engine trouble and had to return to base.

On October 9, after four months of intense activity, No 306 Sqn was told it was to move again. The advance party of 133 Wing HQ proceeded by road in an MT convoy to their new base at Andrews Field, Essex, the winter home of the Mustang Wing. The small convoy of nine vehicles, containing the personnel of the Wing, under the command of the Adjutant of No 129 Sqn, left Brenzett at 2000 hrs on October 10, 1944.

Chapter Six

No 315 (*Deblinski*) Polish Squadron:

Wartime recollections by
Sqn Ldr M Cwynar VM, KW, DFC

FLYING the Mustang Mk.III with No 315 (Polish) Squadron out of Brenzett Advanced Landing Ground, our operational objective was twofold: long-range bomber escorts and, from dawn to dusk, anti-*Diver* patrols (in sections of two aircraft, or singly, intercepting V1 flying-bombs). Our operational perimeter, shared with other fighter squadrons, covered the Dover-Folkestone-Rye coastal line right up to London's balloon barrage.

The V1s, nicknamed 'Doodle-bugs' or 'Buzz Bombs', were launched from the area south of Calais, towards London during the daytime. But to extend the terror, on the odd night, at irregular times, the Germans would send a few over. In the tent, which our CO, Sqn Ldr Horbaczewski, and I shared, listening to those night intruders made us decide to try out a night patrol. We chose a clear, moonless night, thinking it would be easier to detect the 'doodle-bug's' orange-red coloured exhaust flames. We asked our resourceful chief mechanic to prepare the runway's flight path. He had the simple, basic idea of placing a dozen lit oil lamps in a straight line, along the left side of the the Sommerfeld mesh runway.

In the darkness, without the aircraft's positional lights, Horbaczewski got airborne for the approximately two-hour-long patrol. After his safe landing, I took off to continue the night patrol, but we did not intercept any flying-bombs that night. Next day, the airfield commander was not pleased. Horbaczewski had not asked permission; so that was the end of the night flights.

Pilots of No 315 Sqn enjoying the sun and a pause between flying duties. Left to right: F/O T Haczkiewicz, Flt Lt M Cwynar, W/O Jankowski (KIA), F/O J Schmidt (KIA), F/O K Sztramko, F/O K Wunsche. (M Cwynar).

Our successes in shooting down flying-bombs were modest when it came to a comparison with a Tempest squadron stationed nearby. Tempests were not so manoeuvrable as Mustangs, but faster at ground level speed.

To improve the Mustang's ground speed, the

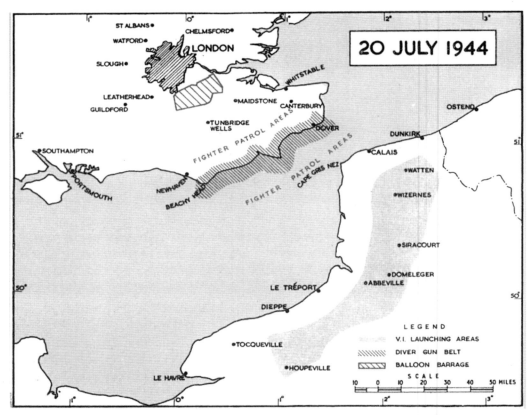

By July 20, 1944, the defences against the V1 had undergone a number of changes compared with the lay-out back in June (see page 11). The gun belt had been redeployed to the coast and the fighters patrolled over the Channel and inland, south of the London balloon barrage.

Merlin engines were given more supercharge, from a maximum 14 lb to 24 lb. The pilots did not like it. At full throttle, we could hear an awful thumping as the connecting rods knocked the pistons without mercy. In the knowledge that one day we were chasing 'buzz bombs' and the next we might be escorting bombers to Norway, we were not keen on 'hammering' our engines.

HQ engineers kept telling us not to worry about the engine – it could be replaced – as long as we were shooting down flying-bombs. That was absolutely true. But, we thought to our-selves, had it occurred to those well-briefed engineers that if the engine packs up when we are flying over a big, very big, stretch of water, replacement will hardly be necessary. There is a more sensible way to obtain that extra speed needed to catch flying-bombs. Knowing at what height 'doodlebugs' went jerking through the air, we patrolled about 1,000 ft above their flight paths. By diving down on them, we gained that extra speed needed to catch up.

At dawn on July 24, we got airborne for an anti-*Diver* patrol. Before we attained sufficient height, we noticed the mushroom shaped explosions of an anti-aircraft artillery barrage over the Folkestone area. The guns were firing at the first series of the morning's flying-bombs. Not having sufficient height, I started to chase one. I was gaining on it, but only slowly. I had to give the engine more revs, but even so it took a while to get to a point 50 yards astern. Once at the proper distance, short bursts of fire were sufficient to damage the flying-bomb's vital component – the gyroscope. Once this part was shot up, the craft veered violently, usually to the left, and dived to the ground.

To give the engine a rest, I throttled back, did a leisurely left turn and observed the impact on the ground. It exploded in what looked like, in the morning mist, an orchard with young trees.

I turned to a south-east direction and pushed the throttle forward to increase speed, but there was no response! The propeller was idling, dri-ven only by the airspeed. At 2,000 ft, I had to

Above: Sqn Ldr E Horbaczewski (second left), CO, No 315 Sqn, poses with his Mustang Mk.III and fellow pilots shortly before his death on August 18, 1944. Extreme left is F/O B J A Nowosielski, and to the right of the C/O are: W/O S Bedowski, not known, W/O T Janowski, not known, Flt Lt M Cwynar, not known. Below: Sqn Ldr E Horbaczewski demonstrates with the aid of W/O T Slon how he rescued fellow pilot Tamowicz from certain capture after crashlanding. (Polish Institute).

look for a suitable landing place, a field where, if the worst came to the worst, I could land with the undercarriage in the 'up' position. Luckily, through the morning mist, I spotted a hangar and that could only mean a permanent airfield. In fact, there were three hangars to the north west at what proved to be West Malling, an RAF night fighter base. With the hydraulics working, the undercarriage and flaps came down and I landed, stopping in the middle of the airfield. The old times came flooding back to my mind, way back in the days when I was learning to fly, and was pleased when I made a neat three-point landing on lush, green grass.

I telephoned Brenzett from the flying control tower. Horbaczewski came over in a jeep, his favourite toy, and brought our chief mechanic, Korczowski. In no time, he found that the throttle linkage had jammed somewhere between the pilot's left hand side in the cabin, and the engine connection. I was soon on my way back to Brenzett.

In the early morning of July 30, nine Mustangs of No 315 Sqn, with Sqn Ldr Eugeniusz Horbaczewski leading, took off from Brenzett with empty, dropable combat fuel tanks (one under each wing). After an hour-long flight, we landed at RAF Coltishall. There, we enjoyed a sumptuous lunch in the Officers' Mess, and then went back to the airfield to wait for the order to take off. Our Mustangs had been refuelled. The dropable combat tanks were also full – they each held 75 US gallons. There was nothing else to do but lay in the shade of the aircrafts' wings and try to relax before what was to be an arduous, five-hour-long flight.

At this point, to explain the purpose of our mission, I must digress. The Allies were receiving reports that the Germans were shipping uranium ore from the Bergen region of Norway, along the coast towards the Kattegat and on to Schweinemünde. To cause disruption, the British were sending light bomber formations to sink anything that moved along the Norwegian coast. The Germans posted one *Staffel* (squadron) of Messerschmitt Bf 109s to Stavanger to protect what was vital traffic to them. Our light bombers, mainly Canadian-flown Beaufighters, were taking heavy losses at the hands of the German fighters. To counter the losses, the RAF High Command decided to surprise the *Luftwaffe* by sending an escort of Mustangs along with the Beaufighters.

During the height of the Campaign, airmen at Brenzett decided to protect themselves from spent ammunition cases and debris from exploding V1s by sleeping and sheltering in concrete pipes. A wise precaution, as there were incidents of airmen being hit whilst in their tented accommodation, not only from debris, but aircraft bullets. Note the large tin of treacle on the box; some things never change. (Polish Institute).

Above: A group of No 315 Sqn pilots being briefed on dive bombing by Armaments Officer. Stifling a yawn at bottom left is W/O T Jankowski, and others facing the camera, clockwise, are F/O K Wunsche, Flt Lt M Cwynar, F/O T Haczkiewicz, Flt Lt H Pietrzak (with pipe). (Polish Institute). Below: Affectionately adopted by members of No 315 Sqn, the actress Virginia Cherril was known as Godmother by the Polish pilots. She is seen here on the left with a female companion during a visit to Brenzett. (K Stembrowicz).

Finally, the orderly arrived from the control tower with the order to get airborne for a rendezvous with the Canadian squadron. We took off, as usual, with the fuel on main tanks behind the pilot's cabin. When escorting bombers at heights of 20,000 ft or more, we always flew for 25-30 minutes on these tanks to make sure we used up a certain amount of fuel. That eliminated the Mustang's adverse lateral instability. This time, however, heading low towards the Wash, north of King's Lynn, we had to change to the dropable combat fuel tanks soon after being airborne. This, as it later transpired, was going to pose some difficulties.

As we approached the Wash, the weather began to close in, with a rainy, warm frontal system approaching from the west. We soon spotted the Beaufighters, in close formation, low down 'on the deck' to avoid radar detection. CO Horbaczewski, with his section of three Mustangs, took up position on the starboard side of the Beaufighters, while I went to port and Maciek Kirste to the rear. The weather worsened rapidly as we closed in on the Beaufighters, forming a tight formation around the Canadians, whose leader kept a steady course while 'hugging the waves'.

Maciek Kirste came through on the radio transmitter to inform our leader that he had lost visual contact with the formation. Horbaczewski ordered him to fly back to England. It was always dangerous in bad weather or while in the clouds to accelerate in an attempt to rejoin a formation after losing visual contact. With only six of us left, we ordered our wingmen to go echelon starboard and port respectively, and, as in cloud formation, held on grimly. We did not dare lose the Canadians, because we had to protect them. After two hours of total concentration, suddenly it was as if we had flown through a curtain or passed over a cliff. There was a complete transformation. We had overtaken the eastern edge of the frontal system. The sun was behind us – a useful tactical advantage – and in front we had the beautiful panoramic view of the Norwegian coast. 'So this is Greig's homeland', I said to myself; but it was not a time to think of music!

A few miles from the land, the Beaufighters turned to the right along the coast in search of

Shortly after D-Day, a No 315 Sqn Mustang III is rearmed. On the right, an armourer checks each round before loading the belt into the wing. This aircraft retains the original cockpit instead of the later 'blown' Malcolm hood which slid rearwards for access. (J Polak).

Ground crew using a cradle to lift a bomb onto the underwing pylon of a Mustang III. (J Polak).

shipping. Behind them and slightly above, Horbaczewski tucked in with his section, while I moved to his right with mine. We changed to the main fuselage fuel tanks and, keenly observing the Norwegian coast, waited. Not to betray our positions in the sun, we still kept our dropable fuel tanks under our wings. Within a few minutes, one of Horbaczewski's wingmen spotted German fighters approaching through a fjord inlet, heading for the Beaufighters. There were two groups of four Bf 109s, leisurely, almost nonchalantly, carrying out a left-hand turn to take up position to attack the Canadians. Jettisoning our wing fuel tanks, we attacked. Horbaczewski went in first, attacking the inner group, and I engaged the outer formation.

They were taken completely by surprise. They turned towards us and, having learned a thing or two in battles over France – they were told the Spitfire, when diving, shuddered, and with us approaching out of the sun, they had not recognised our Mustangs – 'sturzt' towards the sea.

In diving and then climbing in a left-hand turn, I had engaged the group's leader. By the way he was scything through the air, the edges

of his Messerschmitt's wings stitching the sky with air-condensed threads, I realised he was good. He pulled hard, so did I! With the fuselage tank still full and the Mustang's adverse lateral stability, there wasn't much room for imaginative manoeuvring, so I had to hold a steady, smooth turn. With a few hundred revs always in reserve, I held on patiently. For one 360° circle or more, there was stalemate. Then the Mysza/ Michael duo's idea came in useful.

I lowered the flaps 10° and was gaining on him. My solar plexus stopped churning as I felt sure of getting on his tail. But all the time I was thinking, 'pull smoothly; get that extra reserve throttle on'. I got him in my gunsights' illuminated ring, pulled straight through his line of flight, one diameter – two – three diameters of deflection, and then pressed the firing button. For a split second, there was nothing, then I saw the bullets punching holes, first on his tail section and then the fuselage, canopy and wings . . .

The following year, 1945, as Commanding Officer of No 316 (Warsaw) Sqn, I flew the unit to Fairwood Common, South Wales, for air-to-air and air-to-ground gunnery courses. At the pre-course cinema show, a selection of fascinat-

Mustangs prepare for another sortie, these No 315 Sqn aircraft carrying the cockerel marking which formed the unofficial unit badge. Aircraft PK-I was often flown by F/O M Kirste. (Polish Institute).

ing air battles of the war was shown. Somewhere in the Air Ministry Michael's film is gathering dust. Let me explain the Mysza/Michael idea. When converting from Spitfire VBs to Mustangs at ALG Coolham (West Sussex), in April-May 1944, two flight commanders of No 315 Sqn, Henryk Stefankiewicz ('Mysza') and myself, had tried many brainstorming ideas. When engaging the enemy low, over the ground or sea, there was only one manoeuvre at the fighter pilot's disposal – an ideally constructed, yes, constructed, right turn.

When the Mustang's speed dropped to 220-240 mph, by lowering 10° of flaps, the pilot could get on to his opponent's tail in no time. At a safe height, Mysza and I, by alternating the configuration of the Mustangs, proved it really worked.

There was a considerable danger, though.

The Mustang was a great, but unforgiving machine. When the flaps were down, it pulled crudely, and at an even lower speed, say 200, it could stall. When told about our experiment, Horbaczewski would not have it. He told us not to discuss it with the other pilots, saying, 'Flaps or no flaps, I don't want to see my pilots falling from the skies'.

After the engagement off the Norwegian coast which ended in an individual melée, as described already, we tried to gather ourselves together. To save valuable fuel, it was decided we would fly home in two separate sections.

Pilots of No 315 Sqn manage time for a photocall. Note that Horbaczewski, third from left, is wearing an American lifejacket while his companions have the standard RAF issue. (Polish Institute).

Horbaczewski 'inherited' my wingman, Idrian. 'Dziobek's' Bozydar Nowosielski became my companion. We headed home. In no time, we had flown back into the same atrocious weather. It seemed, probably because of the strain, even worse than before. There was water below and water lashing down from above. It is written that 'God created land, sea and the firmament'. There was, as far. as, and much farther than, we could see, only one . . . the sea!

I decided to pay more attention to the flying panel, the instruments. I adjusted the altimeter to zero, came gradually to sea level, approximately 10 ft above the waves, set altimeter to '0' (zero); only now and again did I check to see if the wingmen were still with me, and continued to head for home. Tadek Jankowski, a gifted pilot and trusted wingman, began to pester me: 'Michael! Let's go above the clouds! Let's climb up!' It would have been pleasant to go above, to see the sun and skim over the clouds having a breather. But soon we were to realise that we were in trouble.

I was approaching land through a low cloud base without a clue as to my position or when and where I was going to get down. To have gone above would only have compounded our difficulties. I told Jankowski to keep quiet. Steady Nowosielski did not utter a word.

After reaching the English coastline, I turned south and, to orientate myself, flew along the coast. South of Bridlington, I found an airfield and the three of us landed safely. We spent the night in a comfortable bed, which was a pleasant change from Brenzett's camp bed in the tent. 'Dziobek' Horbaczewski's section landed about 30 miles south of us, near Hull. They also overnighted there. Next day, we flew back to Brenzett to learn that after sinking one merchant ship and setting a few barges on fire, the Canadian Beaufighters returned safely to base. The enemy casualties were eight '109s. Our score: 8-0.

After a successful mission you are exhilarated; you light a cigarette, talk and laugh, and, most importantly, it strengthens friendship with your flying colleagues that remains until your dying day. Mercifully, you never knew whether the following day you might be packing your friend's personal belongings to be kept for relatives in his native land.

Another day, another mission: I took off at 1400 hrs, leading a No 315 Sqn formation on an armed recce to the east side of Cologne, towards Hannover and Hamburg. North of Hannover, flying low, I noticed a large airbase with hangars on the north-west side. As it proved later, with some aircraft inside. It was too late to re-form into echelon position, so, with the leading section only slightly abreast of the others, we strafed the hangars which had the aircraft inside.

Sgt Dzialowski and a fellow airman. In the background, a line of Mustangs on the flightline at Brenzett. (S Dzialowski).

Above: A member of the ground crew leans on the 75 gal drop tank, and two officers listen with some amusement as a bareheaded Flt Lt M Cwynar relates a fighter pilot's story with the usual arm-waving embellishment. Below: A pilot of No 315 Sqn is debriefed after landing back at Brenzett. Under the fuselage are the inner main wheel doors. When the engine was shut down, the hydraulic pressure would hold these doors in the closed position, but as the pressure gradually bled off, the doors would drop open. (Polish Institute).

For a second attack, I decided to place the Mustangs' echelon starboard, at safe distances, and make a more organised job. I was leading and, before opening fire on the targets, met heavy ground flak with tracer bullets whizzing by. To use our jargon, the Germans were 'stitching the sky'.

After strafing the hangars we turned westwards and, to avoid ground fire from the Hamburg conurbations and the periphery of smaller towns, flew south of Bremen towards Holland. Over the Waddersee we set a homeward course for Manston in Kent. Flying westwards through a cloudless sky towards the sun, it felt very warm. My neck particularly felt as if it was burning, as did my face. I took off the R/T and oxygen mask, and started rubbing my face and neck with my left hand, trying to get rid of the 'sweat'.

Flying operationally in sections of four aircraft, we generally kept a loose formation with comfortable distances from each other. Kazik Sztramko, a very experienced pilot, who had been a friend and flying colleague since the days at 113 *Eskadra*, Warsaw Fighter Brigade, and even before, as a flying partner at Sarny in 1938, was my wingman on this flight. He began to edge closer to me, staring into my cabin. Thinking he was just having fun or maybe showing off by demonstrating how close he was able to overlay his Mustang's wing over mine, I

decided to ignore his capering. But he edged closer still, then called me on the R/T: 'Michael, your face is covered with blood. You are wounded. How do you feel?' I replied I felt rather warm, particularly round the face and the right side of my neck, otherwise I was alright. Kazik, as if to protect me, kept close all the way to our base at Brenzett.

Our conversation during the flight, as on all operational flights, had been monitored by Fighter Command operations room. After we landed, the airfield commander, Nowierski (alas, Horbaczewski no more), drove with an ambulance and a doctor straight to my Mustang, PK-Z. What happened was that whilst strafing the hangars north of Hannover, a ground flak bullet entered almost the centre of my cockpit, grazing my neck before exiting at the rear of the sliding canopy. I had been bleeding slightly, but by rubbing my face and neck had smeared the blood over my face, thus making the slight wound appear much worse. I was driven quickly to the doctor's tent, where a small bandage was put round my neck, and I was given an anti-tetanus injection, and discharged. Yet it was, to use a banal metaphor, 'a close shave'. Another two millimetres and an artery could have been severed.

When flying operationally, luck was a very important factor. The pre-destined, biological time clock ticked away . . . mercilessly!

Mustangs of 133 Wing bask in the sun between operations. The aircraft are most probably of No 129 Sqn, as there are no Polish markings on the nose of the aircraft. (Polish Institute).

Sqn Ldr E Horbaczewski. This is one of a number of drawings of Polish aircrew produced during the war by Slawa Sadlowska. (Polish Institute).

Chapter Seven

No 315 (*Deblinski*) Polish Squadron
at Brenzett: July 9 - October 10, 1944
Recollections by F/O Stembrowicz

No 315 Sqn, flying North American Mustang Mk IIIs, landed at ALG Brenzett from RAF Station Ford on July 6, 1944. The squadron, together with No 306 (Polish) and No 129 Sqns, was transferred from 133 Wing, Tactical Air Force (Wing callsign 'OXO') to Air Defence of Great Britain (ADGB) in response to attacks on England by German V1s, which began on June 13, 1944.

From July 1, No 316 (Polish) Sqn, flying from Friston (West Sussex), was also engaged in the fight against the V1 flying-bombs, or to give them their official names, 'Beachcrafts' or 'Divers'. I landed on ALG Brenzett in Mustang III FB184, and flew my first sortie against the *Divers* the next day, lasting 1 hr 35 mins in Mustang FB170. During our stay at Brenzett, I flew Mustangs with the following serial numbers: FZ169, FB382, FX995, SR440, FZ128, FX903 and FB371.

The first V1 was shot down on July 11 by Flt Sgt Jankowski, the second by P/O Swistun; next day P/O Swistun shot down two and Flt Lt Zborzek one. During our stay at Brenzett, P/O Swistun and Flt Sgt Jankowski both destroyed

Above: F/O K Stembrowicz in full flying gear, in front of his aircraft. The small perforated area below the Polish marking is the starboard inspection panel for the air filter.

V1s by tipping them over with the wingtips of their Mustangs, having run out of ammunition.

The patrols against the flying-bombs did not stop the squadron from a variety of other flying duties. On July 23, we escorted RAF Beau-

Aircraft incidents at Brenzett ALG			
Aircraft Type	Serial No	Remarks	Date
Hawker Tempest	JR447	Crashed through trees on north side of main road between Moat House and Tower House; pilot F/O W Parks, No 198 Sqn, Manston, blinded by glycol, thrown clear unconscious; later died at First Aid post, New Romney.	9.3.44
P-47D Thunderbolt		Believed to be 56th FG, 8th USAAF	22.6.44
Hawker Tempest	JN738	Crashlanded at Brenzett. Pilot, Flt Sgt M J A Rose uninjured. No 3 Sqn, RAF, 150 Wing, Newchurch.	23.6.44
B-17 Flying Fortress		Crashed at Brenzett; unit unknown. Buried its nose in hedge along the Ashford road. Towed clear of runway. 8th. USAAF.	10/11.44
Mustang III	FX878	W/O W Siwek, No 315 Sqn. Pilot killed during landing.	13.9.44

fighters on an uneventful 'shipping strike' to the shores of Norway. The previous day, flying Mustang FX903, I shot down my first V1, firing three short bursts from a range of 200 down to 100 yards; the V1 crashed north of Dymchurch, just past the 'Napoleonic' military canal.

On July 30, ten serviceable aircraft of the squadron took off on an escort mission to Norway. Four turned back – one with engine trouble, three because the extremely poor visibility made it very difficult to keep in formation, even a close one. So, six Mustangs only flew on. They were led by the legendary (to the Polish Air Force) Sqn Ldr Eugeniusz Horbaczewski; the other pilots were Flt Lt Cwynar, F/O Nowosielski, P/O Swistun, W/O Jankowski, and W/O Idrian. They escorted 48 Beaufighters on a shipping strike. Some 30 miles from the shore the expedition met, and immediately attacked, 15 German fighters – Messerschmitts and Focke-Wulfs. The Beaufighters had a field day; the port and shipping were attacked, anti-aircraft guns destroyed, the railway station and signal boxes were blown up. In addition, eight German fighters were destroyed and all our aircraft returned safely.

During the month of August, combat missions were freely mixed with V1 patrols and the squadron's score climbed steadily, but nothing spectacular happened until August 18. On that day, the squadron was to carry out *Rodeo 385*, a long-range fighter sweep, Brenzett-

Below: Flt Sgt J Bargielowski taxis out as Sqn Ldr Horbaczewski, left, and P/O Galinski look on. The Sommerfield tracking can clearly be seen. (J Bargielowski).

Polish airmen pose for a photograph while working on Mustang PK-F, serial FB145, of No 315 Sqn, flown on occasion by Flt Lt K Stembrowicz. This aircraft survived the war and was finally taken out of service on March 14, 1946. An account of the pilot's memories of Brenzett can be found in the text. (Polish Institute).

Another in a series of views taken in July 1944 at Brenzett, with the same group of pilots as shown in Chapter Five. Three of these pilots were killed in action in later operations. (M Cwynar).

Le Touquet-Cormeilles-Romilly (east of Paris), at a height of 8,000 ft, and back to base at low level, attacking targets as they presented themselves. Sqn Ldr Horbaczewski led; the other pilots were: *First Section*, F/O Nowosielski, Flt Sgt Bargielowski, Flt Sgt Czerwinski. *Second Section*, Flt Lt Pietrzak, W/O Slon, P/O Swistun, Flt Sgt Siwek. *Third Section*, Flt Lt Schmidt, Flt Sgt Kijak, F/O Kliman, P/O Judek.

Take-off was at 7.30 am. Nothing happened until the Mustangs neared Beauvais, north-east of Paris. There, the squadron met three groups of enemy fighters, taking off or circling at 3,000 ft – some 60 in all. The Mustangs dropped their auxiliary fuel tanks and dived; the Germans scattered. The result of that attack was that 16 Fw 190s were destroyed, one Fw 190 probably destroyed, and three Fw 190s damaged. It was the biggest victory by one squadron ever. Tragically, however, the squadron lost its CO, Sqn Ldr Eugeniusz Horbaczewski, who was shot down after destroy-

The adjutant of 133 Wing with Gp Cpt Nowierski, in their 'office' at Brenzett. Note the field telephone on the table. (Polish Institute).

Sqn Ldr Eugine Horbaczewski checks the Form 700 held by the crew chief before quickly boarding his air-craft, PK-G, FB166. His helmet hangs on the cockpit mirror and covers the gunsight, while along the wing root, a non-slip cloth protects what is already a worn surface and will be removed before the engine is start-ed. Note the marking at the flap hinge which indicates the setting. (J Bargielowski).

ing three Fw 190s. In his flying career he had shot down 16-and-a-half aircraft confirmed, probably destroyed one, and damaged one. He was decorated with the Gold Cross of the Order Virtuti Militari, triple Cross of Valour, the DSO and DFC. He is buried in the local cemetery at Creil in France, Military Section, grave Z379.

The list of individual victories on that remarkable flight was: Sqn Ldr Horbaczewski, three; Flt Lt Pietrzak, two-and-a-half; F/O Nowosielski, one; W/O Slon, one-and-a-half; P/O Swistun, one, and one probable; Flt Sgt Kijak, one destroyed, one damaged; Flt Lt Schmidt, one destroyed; Flt Sgt Bargielowski, two destroyed, and two damaged; Flt Sgt Siwek, three destroyed.

During the remainder of August, September and the early part of October, No 315 Sqn took part in many sorties escorting bombers over Holland and Germany, as well as acting as escort to the glider-towing Halifaxes and Dakotas to Arnhem. With the flying-bombs almost completely defeated, the squadron left Brenzett on October 10, and moved to the RAF base at Andrews Field, near Braintree, Essex.

The squadron shot down 53-and-a-half flying-bombs while based at Brenzett, and the last bomb destroyed by a Polish pilot was on March 25, 1945, when Flt Lt Bibrowicz shot one down over Essex when flying from Andrews Field. The total number of V1s fired against Great Britain was 10,492. Fighters shot down 1,846, anti-aircraft guns 1,878, while barrage balloons accounted for 231, but 2,419 of the V1s reached London. Polish pilots destroyed 190 V1s; just over 10% of all those destroyed by fighters. Over 1,300 were destroyed in Kent.

Above: Surviving today, and on display at the Army Aviation Museum, Oakey, Australia, is this Auster Mk. 3, serial No NK126. This aircraft was used for Communications Flights at Brenzett and on more than one occasion was flown from Brenzett by Sqn Ldr P D Thompson DFC, who was CO, No 129 Sqn from July 1944 until April 1945. (Museum of Army Aviation).

Auster communications aircraft used at Brenzett

Aircraft Serial No.	Squadron	Remarks	Arrival Date
MZ254	306	Crashed, Southbourne, Sussex Pilot W/O M Machowiak killed	22.7.44
MZ125	306	Sold to RNeth AF, 23.4.46	25.8.44
MZ180	306	Crashed at Tidworth, Hants, 3.10.44	24.8.44
NZ229	133 Wing	Sent to Netherlands, SOC 5.49	8.7.44
NX500	315	Still flying in 1989 and flew with No 656 Air Op Sqn, Westenhanger, Nr Lympne, 21.4.44	
NK126	129	Flown by Sqn Ldr P H Thompson DFC, CO, No 129 *Mysore* Sqn, RAF	8.7.44
MK299	129	As above.	7.44

Chapter Eight

No 122 Sqn RAF: Operations from ALG Brenzett, 1943, and pilot profiles

THIS squadron moved to Brenzett ALG temporarily to enable the Works Service Corps to repair the roads and runways at Kingsnorth ALG, where they served from July to October 1943. The extracts below are taken from the squadron's Operational Record Book during its few days at Brenzett.

September 14: Weather, cloudy. All serviceable aircraft were airborne at 0820 hrs, and moved to the ALG at Brenzett, approx 7 miles south of the airfield. To enable the Works Service Corps to repair the roads and runways at Kingsnorth Airfield, formation flying was carried out from the ALG during the day. At 1730 hrs, the squadron was airborne along with Nos 19 and 65 Sqns as high cover to 72 Marauders bombing Lille, but was recalled when over the Channel owing to bad weather over the target. The squadron landed at Brenzett at 1800 hrs.

Right: Post D-Day, Mustangs are re-armed for another mission, PK-M in the foreground and PK-X behind. Bombs have been delivered from the dump for loading.

September 15: Weather, overcast. Formation flying practice was carried out during the day. At 1800 hrs, the squadron was airborne with Nos 19 and 65 Sqns as withdrawal cover to 40 Liberators which had bombed Rouen. No

An aerial view of Brenzett ALG taken shortly after the war, in 1945. The runways are clearly visible, as are four blister hangars used by 133 Wing. The Ashford Road is to the left, with Ivychurch village to the right of the airstrip. Spring Farm is seen to the right of the runway in the centre of the picture. Sadly, none of the hangars exist, no doubt dismantled shortly after this photo was taken. (Brenzett Aeronautical Museum Trust).

enemy aircraft were encountered; the squadron returned to base at 1935 hrs. Aircraft (Spitfire IXs) and pilots involved were: MH317, Sqn Ldr Wickham; MH380, P/O Gilbert; MH368, F/O Innes; MH318, Flt Sgt Niesh; MA746, Flt Lt MacIntyre; MH382, P/O Cush; MH379, Flt Lt Inness; MA803, Flt Sgt MacCaffery; MA846, Cpt Johnsen; MH373, Flt Sgt Bennett; MH382, P/O Lawson; BS272, F/O Pavey.

One of the most decorated of aces' aircraft was that of Sqn Ldr Horbaczewski, PK-G, FB166. Here, a member of the Polish groundcrew puts the finishing touches to the fourth V1 'kill'. The circular hole is for the flare pistol. (Polish Institute).

September 16: Weather, overcast early in the morning. Air-to-air firing was carried out during the day. The squadron was airborne at 1650 hours with Nos 19 and 65 Sqns as high cover to 72 Marauders bombing Beamont-le-Roger. Some enemy aircraft were seen, but dived away when the Wing turned to attack.

The squadron returned to RAF Kingsnorth at 1835 hrs. The runways and roads were made serviceable by 1800 hrs and all aircraft and personnel returned to their usual home base.

The Spitfire IXs and their pilots on this escort duty were: MA836, Sqn Ldr Wickham; MA757, Flt Sgt Hunter; MH375, F/O Edwards; MH368, Flt Lt Adams; MA746, Flt Lt MacIntyre; MA803, Flt Sgt Oakley; BS192, P/O Gilbert; MH379, F/O Charney; MA846, Cpt Johnsen; MH317, F/O Stephens; MH383, P/O Lawson; MH318, Flt Sgt Bennett.

Sqn Ldr Eugeniusz Horbaczewski, DSO, DFC

On July 30, 1944, while escorting Beaufighters off the Norwegian coast, Sqn Ldr Horbaczewski led six Mustangs of No 315 Sqn against approximately 20 enemy aircraft, attacking in a brave and skilful manner. In the course of the engagement, eight enemy aircraft were destroyed without loss; Sqn Ldr Horbaczewski himself accounted for one-and-a-half aircraft.

On August 18, 1944, whilst leading his squadron, he sought out and engaged a total of some 60 Fw 190s which were in the process of taking off from an airfield in the Beauvais area, and assembling for an operation in strength. In the dogfight which ensued at 2,000 ft, and which lasted for 15 minutes, the Mustangs shot down 16 Fw 190s, probably destroyed one more, and damaged three others, for the loss of one pilot, Sqn Ldr Horbaczewski, who did not return. On August 29, 1944, Sqn Ldr Horbaczewski was awarded the Distinguished Service Order. Of the total of 16 aircraft destroyed in the Beauvais area, Sqn Ldr Horbaczewski had accounted for three Fw 190s. That morning, his fellow pilots had advised him not to fly, as he had complained of feeling unwell.

This epic air battle was another example of the brilliant leadership, determination, courage and fighting ability of this lion-hearted Polish officer in his unceasing endeavours to seek out and destroy the enemy. Since he was awarded the DFC, he had flown a total of approximately 250 hours on operations, and had destroyed a further eight-and-a-half enemy aircraft and

Above: In the background is Mustang PK-G, the aircraft flown by Sqn Ldr Horbaczewski; it is possible that on this occasion it was flown by another pilot, as the C/O is not in his flying gear. The pilot in the centre is Flt Lt M Cwynar; the other two are W/O T Jankowski and W/O Beczynski. Below: The CO taxis out to take off and formate with other aircraft over Romney Marsh for another mission. Horbaczewski was very popular with his fellow pilots and groundcrew. He was affectionately nicknamed 'Little Beak' from his school days, possibly because he was rather short in stature. (Polish Institute).

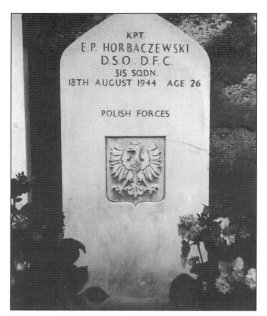

KPT
E.P. HORBACZEWSKI
D.S.O. D.F.C.
315 SQDN.
18TH AUGUST 1944   AGE 26

POLISH FORCES

Horbaczewski now lies buried in grave Z379 in the Military Section of the Creil cemetery, just north of Paris. Beneath a fine portrait of this much loved and gallant officer are arranged his medals and decorations at the Sikorski and Polish Museum, London. (War Graves Commission).

four-and-a-half flying-bombs. He carried out 27 armed reconnaissances with bombs, 32 bomber escorts over Germany, 15 fighter sweeps, and 55 patrols over Sicily and Galerno Beanice.

Born on September 28, 1917, at Kiev, Ukraine, he joined the Polish Air Force in 1937 and was known as 'Little Beak'. He did not claim any victories during the Polish Campaign, but later escaped to Britain, where he was posted to No 303 Sqn. Later, he joined No 145 Sqn ('Skalski's Circus') in North Africa, flying Spitfires. He emerged as the top scorer in Tunisia, and later took command of No 43 Sqn during the invasion of Italy. On return to the UK, he assumed command of No 315 Sqn, which by then was flying Mustang IIIs.

The incident for which Sqn Ldr Horbaczewski will perhaps be best remembered took place shortly after D-Day when 133 Wing was at Coolham, Sussex. He was leading an attack on German tanks in Normandy when he saw Tamowicz, who had been hit by flak, make a forced landing on marshy land. Some Americans were already clearing a landing strip not far away and, although it was still too short for use, the Sqn Ldr put his Mustang down on it. Borrowing a jeep from the same, astonished, Americans, he drove to the edge of the marsh,

got out and waded into the muddy water. At times, he sunk up to his chest, but he struggled on until he reached the Mustang. The pilot lay wounded in the cockpit and, helping him out, Horbaczewski half dragged, half carried him back through the marsh to the jeep and set off for his own aircraft. He threw out his own parachute from his seat to make more room, lifted the wounded pilot into the cockpit, got in himself, settled down on the other pilot's knees, and took off. Back at base, astonished airmen watched as the Mustang landed and two pilots emerged from the cockpit!

Sqn Ldr Stanislaw Skalski, DSO, DFC, PVM, CofV

Born in Russia in 1915, Stanislav Skalski joined the Polish Air Force in 1936 and joined No 142 Sqn; in September 1939, he escaped to the UK. He was commissioned in the RAF in January 1940 and joined No 302 Sqn on August 3; on August 12 he moved to No 501 Sqn, Gravesend. He was shot down by Bf 109s over Canterbury and was injured, remaining in Herne Bay Hospital for several weeks. After being awarded the VM (5th class) on February 1, 1941, he was posted to No 306 Sqn at Tern Hill on February 25, 1941.

In October, he was posted to 58 OTU, Grangemouth, as an instructor; he was awarded two Bars to his KW, and in February 1942, the DFC. He then joined No 316 Sqn as 'B' Flight Commander, and in June he took command of No 317 Sqn, also at Northolt. Awarded a Bar to his DFC, he then went to 58 OTU Balado Bridge as Chief Flying Instructor. Skalski went with other Polish pilots to the Middle East, where they formed the Polish Fighter Team known as 'Skalski's Circus', attached to No 145 Sqn. By May 12, 1942, he had destroyed some 30 enemy aircraft.

In July 1943, he joined No 601 Sqn at Luqa, Malta, as CO. Returning to the UK in October, he was awarded a second Bar to his DFC, and became Wing Leader of 131 Wing at Northolt on December 13. He was transferred as Wing Leader to 133 Wing on April 11, 1944, leaving them at Brenzett on July 12.

For a short time, Skalski was at the Command and General Staff School in Kansas, returning to HQ 11 Group as Wing Commander. He was awarded the DSO on May 26, 1945. In 1947, he returned to Poland and headed the Fighter Command, Polish Air Force. He was later imprisoned by the Russians, and was not released until 1956, when he was put in charge of the Polish Aero Clubs.

Chapter Nine

RAF squadrons at
Brenzett Advanced Landing Ground,
1943-1944

A typical scene on any airfield during wartime, as airmen que up for refreshments from the 'chuck wagon'. During such a break it was not unusual for a V1 to pass overhead, which would send everyone running for cover. (Polish Institute).

No 129 (Mysore) Squadron, RAF

During the First World War, this squadron served at Duxford as a training unit and was reformed as a fighter squadron on June 16, 1941, at Leconfield, flying Spitfire Mk Is. It became fully operational on July 24, and shortly afterwards joined the Tangmere Wing whose job was to escort bombers to the continent.

The squadron continued on this type of operation until November, when it moved to the east coast to protect convoys. The following year, No

129 was back on escorts, scrambles and *Rhubarbs* from its base on the south coast. By May, the squadron was on anti-*Rhubarb* patrols against the Fw 190s and Bf 109s which flew 'hit and run' raids on Kent and Sussex coastal towns. During Operation *Jubilee* (the raid on Dieppe), No 129 attacked gun batteries, flew convoy cover and escorted Hurricanes. Moving to the north of England, it did not see action again until the following February. Throughout 1943, its main role remained that of escort to many daylight raids. After a brief spell at Hornchurch, the squadron again moved north for a well-earned rest.

In March 1944, the squadron's role changed to ground-attack, shortly after it moved to north Wales to convert to the Mustang III, on which it flew its first mission, to Beauvais, on April 26. Soon after D-Day, No 129 was diverted to Brenzett ALG to counter the V1 threat, joining the two Polish squadrons. By September 3, the squadron had destroyed no fewer than 66 flying-bombs. After its success against Hitler's new weapon, the squadron's role changed to that of long-range escort. Its last mission provided cover for the landings on Guernsey in May 1945. On September 1, 1946, the squadron was renumbered No 257 Sqn at Church Fenton.

The squadron's motto was: 'I will defend the right'. The squadron's badge depicts the Ghunda of Mysore, as the unit was the Gift Squadron of the Mysore province in India.

No 129 (Mysore) Sqn served at the following bases:

Leconfield	Jun 1941 - Aug 1941
Westhampnett	Aug 1941 - Nov 1941
Debden	Nov 1941 - Dec 1941
Westhampnett	Dec 1941 - July 1942
Thorney Island	Jul 1942 - Sep 1942
Grimsetter	Sep 1942 - Jan 1943
Detached to Sumburgh & Skeabrae	
Skeabrae	Jan 1942 - Feb 1943
Ibsley	Feb 1943
Tangmere	Feb 1943 - Mar 1943
Ibsley	Mar 1943 - Jun 1943
Hornchurch	Jun 1943 - Jan 1944
Peterhead	Jan 1944 - Mar 1944
Heston	Mar 1944
Llanbedr	Mar 1944 - Apr 1944
Coolham	Apr 1944 - Jun 1944
Holmesley South	Jun 1944
Ford	Jun 1944 - Jul 1944
Brenzett	Jul 1944 - Oct 1944
Andrews Field	Oct 1944 - Dec 1944
Bentwaters	Dec 1944 - May 1945
Dyce	May 1945
Vaernes	Jun 1945 - Aug 1945
Gardemoen	Aug 1945 - Nov 1945
Molesworth	Nov 1945 - Dec 1945
Hutton Cranswick	Dec 1945 - May 1946
Lubeck	May 1946 - Jul 1946
Church Fenton	Jul 1946 - Sep 1946

Commanding Officers:

Sqn Ldr D L Armitage	Jun 1941 - Sep 1941
Sqn Ldr R J Abrahms	Sep 1941 - Jan 1942
Sqn Ldr R H Thomas	Jan 1942 - Sep 1942

Looking across the turning into Moor Lane, which crossed the airfield during the war. A blister hangar was located close to this corner, and pegs which held down the Sommerfield track can still be found in the ploughed field. (Author).

Sqn Ldr H A C Gonay
          Sep 1942 - Sep 1943
Sqn Ldr P V K Tripe (RCAF)
          Sep 1943 - Nov 1943
Sqn Ldr C Haw, DFM, Order of Lenin
          Nov 1943 - Jul 1944
Sqn Ldr P D Thompson, DFC
          Jul 1944 - Apr 1945
Sqn Ldr K C M Giddings, DFC
          Apr 1945 - Jan 1946
Sqn Ldr Wright   Jan 1946
Sqn Ldr Counter, DFC
          Feb 1946 - Jun 1946
Sqn Ldr E Garrad-Cole
          Jun 1946 - Sep 1946

Squadron identified by the code letters 'DV'

Pilots of No 129 (Mysore) Sqn RAF Brenzett, July 10 - October 10, 1944:
Sqn Ldr P D Thompson, DFC C/O
Flt Lt D S Strachan
F/O L G Lunn
Flt Lt A C Leigh
Flt Lt R G Kleimeyer
P/O E W Edwards

F/O J E Hartley
Flt Lt J P Bassett
Sgt R Sandever
Flt Lt K C Baker
Flt Lt D F Ruchwaldy
W/O R E Redhead
W/O R L Thomas
W/O T Hetherington
F/O P A Nicholson
F/O F H Holmes
F/O A F Osborne
P/O J L Bilodeau
P/O A B Thomson
P/O G R Dickson
F/O M Twomey
F/O M Humphries
F/O P N Howard
F/Lt R J Conroy
W/O A J Foster
F/Lt G C Green
F/O D C Parker
Flt Sgt W A Jeal
F/O I G Wood
Flt Sgt A Guest
F/O J N Bertrand

No 315 (Deblinski) Polish Sqn, RAF

This Polish squadron was formed in the RAF at Acklington on February 21, 1941. Flying Hurricanes, it moved to Liverpool and by mid-March was operational; its role was to patrol coastal waters and protect convoys in and out of the Mersey. Its first combat came on May 24 when a Ju 88 was attacked, but the result was inconclusive. In July, No 315 moved to Northolt and started to fly *Rodeos*. Although they shot down two aircraft, claimed three probables and damaged three others, the squadron lost three pilots. Later, flying Spitfires, the action intensified with fighter sweeps, *Ramrods* and *Rhubarbs*. In November, five pilots were lost over Dunkirk, shot down by enemy flak. The squadron was moved back to the Mersey on April 1 for a short rest and was

Sqn Ldr E Horbaczewski, seventh from left, surrounded by fellow pilots and groundcrew of No 315 Sqn. (Polish Institute).

Above: Bombing-up FB145 of No 315 Sqn. This aircraft is believed to have been the oldest machine in the squadron, until it crashed on July 22, 1944. (Dr P Koniarek). Sqn Ldr Michael Cwynar VM, KW, DFC (right) joined the Polish Air Force in 1933 and destroyed two enemy aircraft before escaping to Britain, where he claimed 4.5 aircraft and three V1s. He was CO of No 316 (City of Warsaw) Sqn in 1945. (M Cwynar). Below left: Flt Lt J Polak, of No 315 Sqn. (B Nowosielski).

Russian-born Sqn Ldr Stanislaw Skalski. (Polish Institute).

became escort to transport and glider-towing formations on their way to Holland. By way of a rest, No 315 Sqn moved to Scotland to take on coastal patrol work, patrolling as far afield as Norway.

By 1945, the squadron was escorting bombers well into the heart of Nazi Germany as the war reached its climax. The last mission flown by the squadron was to escort Lancasters to Berchtesgaden on April 25, 1945. In December 1946, the unit disbanded at RAF Coltishall.

then involved in defensive patrols. During this period they destroyed two Ju 88s and damaged another, with the loss of one pilot.

Returning to Northolt in September, they again found themselves flying *Rodeos* and *Ramrods*, although bad weather and the onset of winter hindered and limited the operations. After suffering the loss of four pilots in combat with Fw 190s, the squadron moved north again, flying south to Coltishall and West Malling on occasion.

Not until November 1943, when No 315 Sqn moved south, did the weather slow the pace down. In March 1944, after a few more sorties flying Spitfires, the squadron was re-equipped with the Mustang III. Initially, they flew escort to bomber missions and activity was intense during this period before D-Day; in July, the squadron was deployed for the destruction of the V1, moving to Romney Marsh and joining 133 Wing at Brenzett ALG. Occasionally they were involved in escort missions and, on one occasion, No 315 encountered 15 enemy aircraft and destroyed eight of them.

On August 18, the C/O was killed when the squadron was attacked by 60 Fw 190s; however, 16 enemy aircraft were destroyed and three claimed as damaged. In September, the defensive anti-*Diver* patrols were dropped and No 315 Sqn again returned to its original job of escorting bombers. As well as this role during Operation *Market Garden*, the squadron

No 315 (Deblinski) Polish Sqn served at the following bases:

Acklington	Jan 1941 - Mar 1941
Speke	Mar 1941 - Jul 1941
Northolt	Jul 1941 - Apr 1942
Woodvale	Apr 1942 - Sep 1943
Detached to Valley	
Northolt	Sep 1943 - Jun 1943
Hutton Cranswick	Jun 1943
Ballyhalbert	Jul 1943 - Nov 1943
Heston	Nov 1943 - Apr 1944
Coolham	Apr 1944 - Jun 1944
Holmesley South	Jun 1944
Ford	Jun 1944 - Jul 1944
Brenzett	Jul 1944 - Oct 1944
Andrews Field	Oct 1944
Coltishall	Oct 1944 - Nov 1944
Peterhead	Nov 1944 - Jan 1945
Andrews Field	Jan 1945 - Aug 1945
Coltishall	Aug 1945 - Nov 1945
Fairwood Common	Nov 1945 - Dec 1945
Coltishall	Dec 1945 - Dec 1946

Disbanded at Coltishall on December 6, 1946.

Commanding Officers:

Sqn Ldr H D Cooke Jan 1941 - Jun 1941
Sqn Ldr Pietraszkiewicz
                     Jun 1941 - Sep 1941
Sqn Ldr Szczesniewski
                     Sep 1941 - Nov 1941
Sqn Ldr S Janus, VM, DFC
                     Nov 1941 - May 1942

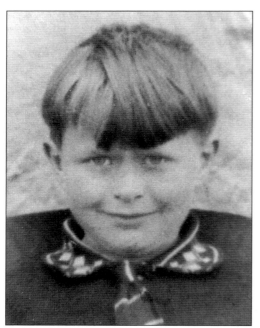

Above: A regular visitor to the ALG at Brenzett was Ian Reid, a young schoolboy whose parents owned the village store. He was befriended by W/O Slon and Sqn Ldr Horbaczewski. On the day the Wing moved from Brenzett, Ian arrived at the airstrip carrying his rucksack, hoping they would take him with them! (T Slon).

Sqn Ldr M Wiorkiewicz
                 May 1942 - Oct 1942
Sqn Ldr T Sawicz   Oct 1942 - Apr 1943
Sqn Ldr J Poplawski, DFC
                 Apr 1943 - Feb 1944
Sqn Ldr E Horbaczewski, DSO
                 Feb 1944 - Aug 1944
Sqn Ldr T Andersz   Sep 1944 - Apr 1945
Sqn Ldr W Potocki   Apr 1945 - Feb 1946
Sqn Ldr J Sieierski   Feb 1946 - Dec 1946

Squadron identified by the code letters 'PK'

Pilots of No 315 (Deblinski) Polish Sqn, RAF Brenzett, July-October 1944:
Sqn Ldr E Horbaczewski C/O, DSO, DFC
F/O H Kirste
Flt Sgt B Czerwinski
Flt Sgt S Bedkowski
F/O K Stembrowicz
F/O A Czerwinski
F/O H Kirste
F/O K Wunsche
P/O B Nowosielski
Flt Lt J Schmidt
F/O T Hackiewicz
Flt Sgt T Jankowski
F/O K Sztramko
Flt Lt M Cwynar, DFC
F/O B Smidowicz
Flt Sgt K Siwek
F/O S Skalski, DSO, DFC
Flt Lt F Wiza
P/O A Judek
Flt Sgt A Ciundziewicki
W/O A Seredyn
Flt Lt J Polak
P/O G Swistun
Flt Sgt R Idrian
Flt Sgt T Slon
Flt Lt H Pietrzak, DFC
F/O P Kliman
Flt Lt J Zbrosek
Flt Sgt J B Bargielowski, DFM
Flt Sgt T Berka
Flt Sgt K Kijak
Flt Sgt J K Donocik
Flt Lt S Blok
Flt Sgt A Syborski
Sgt M Cempel
Sgt B Skladzien
Sqn Ldr J Zulikowski
Sqn Ldr M Wiorkiewicz
P/O M Zaleski
W/O J Zumbach
F/O H Bibrowicz
Sqn Ldr T Andersz
Sgt A Richter

No 306 (Torunski) Polish Sqn, RAF

This squadron, like No 315, was also formed at Church Fenton in August 1940, its first C/O being British; it was the third Polish-manned fighter squadron to serve with the RAF. Moving to Tern Hill, they became operational in November of that year, though they were not very active until 1941 when, in February, they began night patrols. Then, in April, their first Polish C/O led them on Blenheim escorts and fighter sweeps. In May, they returned to night patrols, their first victory falling to F/O Nowak, who destroyed an He 111. They then returned to escort sorties. The squadron converted to Spitfire IIBs and engaged in daylight sweeps and *Ramrods*.

After much activity in 1941, they went north to rest, but two months later returned to escort bombers raiding the Brest area. During April 1942, they met Fw 190s for the first time, destroying one, damaging another, but losing one pilot. The squadron lost four pilots on

The Fleur de Lis

Below: The crossroads in Brenzett, with the Fleur de Lis public house, a 'watering hole' often frequented by the airmen from the strip. (W Smith)

The Bell Inn

Above: Another "home-from-home" was the Bell Inn at Ivychurch (right). (W Smith)

August 22 during intensive *Rhubarb* operations. Although the squadron moved north in March 1943, they flew south to take part in *Ramrod* raids.

In April 1944, the squadron converted to Mustang Mk IIIs, becoming operational in April and flying 310 missions by the end of May. During the invasion of Normandy in June 1944, it carried out reconnaissance missions with bombs; losses were heavy and in July they were transferred to the ALG at Brenzett, forming 133 Wing with Nos 315 and 306 Sqns on anti-*Diver* patrols.

Continuing with long-range escort missions, No 306 Sqn remained with Fighter Command until it was disbanded in January 1947 at RAF Coltishall.

No 306 (Torunski) Sqn served at the following bases:

Church Fenton	Aug 1940 - Nov 1940
Tern Hill	Nov 1940 - Apr 1941
Northolt	Apr 1941 - Oct 1941
Speke	Oct 1941 - Dec 1941
Church Fenton	Dec 1941 - May 1942
Kirton-in-Lindsey	May 1942 - Jun 1942
Northolt	Jun 1942 - Mar 1943
Hutton Cranswick	Mar 1943 - May 1943
Catterick	May 1943 - Aug 1943
Detached to Thornaby	
Gravesend	Aug 1943
Friston	Aug 1943 - Sep 1943
Heston	Sep 1943 - Dec 1943
Llanbedr	Dec 1943 - Jan 1944
Heston	Jan 1944 - Mar 1944
Coolham	Apr 1944 - Jun 1944
Holmesley South	Jun 1944
Ford	Jun 1944 - Jul 1944
Brenzett	Jul 1944 - Oct 1944
Andrews Field	Oct 1944 - Aug 1945
Coltishall	Aug 1945 - Oct 1945
Fairwood Common	Oct 1945 - Nov 1945
Coltishall	Nov 1945 - Jan 1947

Commanding Officers:

Sqn Ldr D R Scott	Aug 1940 - Dec 1940
Sqn Ldr D E Gillam, DFC, AFC	Dec 1940 - Mar 1941
Sqn Ldr T H Rolski	Mar 1941 - Jul 1941
Sqn Ldr J Zaremba	Jul 1941 - Aug 1941
Sqn Ldr J Slonski, VM	Aug 1941
Sqn Ldr A Wozelik	Sep 1941 - Apr 1942
Sqn Ldr T Czerwinski, KW	Apr 1942 - Aug 1942
Sqn Ldr K Ruthowski, DFC	Aug 1942 - Mar 1943
Sqn Ldr W Karkwowski	Mar 1943 - Jan 1944
Sqn Ldr S Lapka	Jan 1944 - Apr 1944
Sqn Ldr J Marciniak	Jun 1944
Sqn Ldr P Niemiec	Jun 1944 - Sep 1944

The husband of Doris Jemison, on his Fordson tractor which he used to maintain the grass on Brenzett ALG. To this day, Doris, who was one of the Brenzett Land Army girls, runs the Red Lion *public house at Snargate, which she and her husband owned. A smashing pint! (Mrs D Jemison).*

Above: A short distance from the Aeronautical Museum at Brenzett is Spring Farm, located on the site of the ALG. (A J Moor).

Sqn Ldr J Zulikowski
Sep 1944 - May 1945
Sqn Ldr J Jeka, DFM
May 1945 - May 1946
Sqn Ldr T Andersz   May 1946 - Jan 1947

Squadron identified by the code letters 'UZ'

Pilots of No 306 (Torunski) Sqn, Brenzett ALG, July-October 1944:
Flt Lt K Marscall
P/O E Zygmund
P/O J Smigielski
Flt Sgt S Rudowski
Flt Sgt J Pomietlarz
P/O F Migos
Flt Sgt S Zudowski
P/O Z Kawnik
Sqn Ldr P Niemic
Flt Sgt F Dowgalski
Sgt A Grodynski
F/O E Tomzak
Flt Sgt S Letki
Flt Sgt J Zaworski
Flt Sgt Z Bezwukio
Flt Lt G Sologub
W/O J Pogowski
P/O S Tronczynski
W/O W Krupa
Flt Lt J Siekierski
F/O G Gierycz

Gp Cpt Rolski
Flt Lt A Beyer
Flt Lt M Wedzik
Flt Sgt N Kolosczyk
Sqn Ldr A Zulikowski
Gp Cpt W Nowierski
Sgt A Szostakowski
F/O J Biazskorski
W/O M Machowiak
Flt Sgt K Michaikiewicz
P/O C Hryniewiecki
Sgt E Hanka
Flt Lt J Schmidt
Flt Lt M Wisiorek
Flt Sgt J Czezowski
Flt Sgt Z Zalenski
P/O W Potocki, DFC
Flt Lt M Gorzula
F/O T Turek
P/O J Bzowski
F/O I Loszkiewicz
W/O W Nowoczyn
F/O H Pietrazak
P/O K Wacnik
Flt Lt K Sporny
Flt Lt B Kudrewicz
Flt Lt C Jaworowski
W/O E Loska
W/O J Rogowski
Flt Sgt W Mrowowski

Missions flown by No 133 Wing, Brenzett ALG, September-October 1944:

3 Sep   Ramrod 1258
        Escort Halifax sqns to Venlo
5 Sep   Armed recce
        Rotterdam-Alphen
6 Sep   Ramrod 1263
        Escort mission
8 Sep   Ranger patrol
        Osnabruck-Oldenburg
10 Sep Fighter sweep
        Rotterdam
11 Sep Ramrod 1269
        Kamen-Castrop

12 Sep Ramrod 1274
        Escort Halifax sqns Wanne-Eickel
13 Sep Ramrod 1280
        Escort Halifax sqns Osnabruck
16 Sep Ranger patrol
        Düsseldorf-Cologne
17 Sep Operation *Market Garden*
        Anti-flak patrol
18 Sep Operation *Market Garden*
        Anti-flak patrol
20 Sep Operation *Market Garden*
        Anti-flak patrol
21 Sep Operation *Market Garden*
        Anti-flak patrol

23 Sep	Operation *Market Garden*	31 Sep	Ramrod 1304
	Anti-flak patrol		Escort bombers to Gosh
25 Sep	Ramrod 1295	2 Oct	Rodeo 405
	Escort bombers to Arnhem		Achmer-Paderborn
26 Sep	Operation *Market Garden*	5 Oct	Ramrod 1313
	Target cover		Aurich
27 Sep	Ramrod 1267	6 Oct	Ramrod 1318
	Escort Halifax sqns to Sterkrade		Gladbach-Cologne
28 Sep	Ramrod 1299	7 Oct	Ramrod 1316
	Escort bombers to Emmerich		Escort Lancasters on Kembs
30 Sep	Ramrod 1302		dam raid
	Escort bombers to Sterkrade		

Above: Today, little evidence remains of the ALG at Brenzett. However, this bridge over a ditch to the fields is original. Back in July 1944, it strained under the weight of RAF trucks arriving with supplies and equipment for 133 Wing. (A J Moor). Below: The memorial unveiled at Brenzett Museum on Sunday, August 7, 1994. It commemorates the 50th Anniversary of D-Day and the V1 Campaign, and the squadrons and units based on the 12 Advanced Landing Grounds in Kent during 1943 and 1944. (A J Moor).

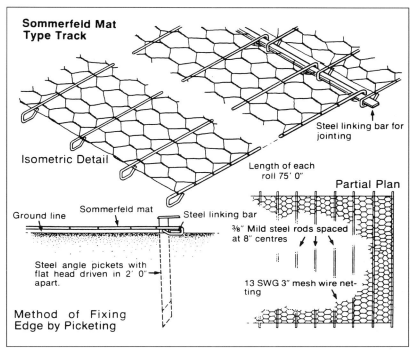

Sommerfeld Mat Type Track

Isometric Detail

Steel linking bar for jointing

Length of each roll 75' 0"

Partial Plan

Ground line   Sommerfeld mat   Steel linking bar

3/8" Mild steel rods spaced at 8" centres

Steel angle pickets with flat head driven in 2' 0" apart.

13 SWG 3" mesh wire netting

Method of Fixing Edge by Picketing

Sommerfeld Tracking, used to reinforce temporary airstrips, was used extensively by RAF Construction Units. Later, with the arrival of the US 9th Air Force, much of this was replaced by Pierced Steel Planking (PSP), preferred by the Americans; sections of both types of tracking may still be found on farmland today.

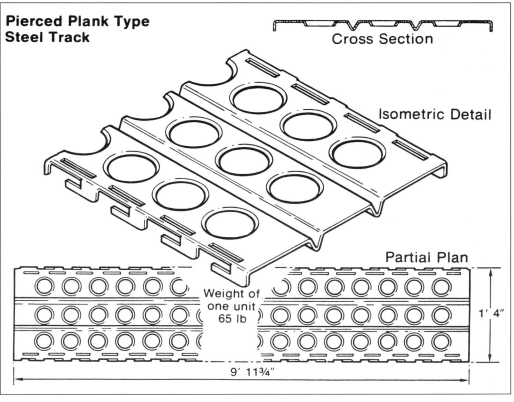

Pierced Plank Type Steel Track

Cross Section

Isometric Detail

Partial Plan

Weight of one unit 65 lb

1' 4"

9' 11¾"

Details of Mustang Mk IIIs of 133 Wing 84 Group lost June - October 1944

Aircraft No	Squadron	Remarks	Date
FB398	315	Missing from sweep over Normandy	22.06.44
FX873	306	Missing, presumed shot down near Dreux	24.06.44
FX878	315	Crashed on approach, Brenzett	13.09.44
FX896	306	Shot down by fighters near Arnhem	17.09.44
FX959	129	Missing from sweep	07.06.44
FX960	315	Hit by flak and abandoned over Norway	10.06.44
FX970	306	Missing near Dreux	23.06.44
FX983	129	Missing, presumed shot down by enemy aircraft near Arnhem	25.09.44
FX994	306	Missing	10.06.44
FZ121	129	Shot down by flak south of Cherbourg	22.06.44
FZ144	306	Missing near Dreux	23.06.44
FZ147	315	Missing near Evreux	24.06.44
FZ156	306	Missing near Montford	07.06.44
FZ157	315	Missing	21.06.44
FZ163		Missing near Dreux	23.06.44
FZ176	129	Hit by flak and crashlanded	17.06.44
FZ189	306	Missing near Montford	07.06.44
FZ196	306	Crashed into sea off North Foreland, Kent	27.09.44
FZ197	306	Missing near Montford	07.06.44
HB840	315	Engine cut out; belly landed in field, Park Wood, Surrey	28.07.44
HB871	306	Swung on take-off and hit gully, Friston	22.09.44
FB108	129	Missing near Vire	10.06.44
FB138	129	Engine cut out; crashlanded five miles north of Antwerp	27.09.44
FB139	306	Missing from sweep	07.06.44
FB147	129	Missing, presumed shot down by fighters near Arnhem	25.09.44
FB148	129	Shot down by flak near Appledore	09.09.44
FB151	306	Missing from escort to Emmerich	27.09.44
FB165	129	Hit trees on take-off at Coolham	17.06.44
FB168	306	Crashed during attack on barges, Seine	07.08.44
FB169	129	Bomb dropped off while taxying, damaged aircraft, at Coolham	15.06.44
FB174	317	Damaged by Bf 109s off Norway	30.07.44
FB183	129	Struck off charge	04.09.44
FB315	315	Damaged by Bf 109s off Norwegian coast. Struck off charge	30.07.44
FB183	129	Struck off charge	04.09.44
FB188	315	Hit by flak and abandoned over Normandy	10.06.44
FB196	306	Missing	28.06.44
FB206	306	Collided with Spitfire NH 713 and crashed, 1.5 miles west of Ham Street	18.08.44
FB230	315	Undercarriage retracted on take-off, Bognor Regis	05.08.44
FB241	306	Shot down by AA while chasing V1 three miles south of Hastings	29.07.44
FB346	129	Hit tree, forced landing, Kempston, Beds	27.07.44
FB355	315	Missing on sweep	18.08.44
FB367	315	Missing	20.09.44
FB389	129	Abandoned over Zuid Beveland	18.10.44
FB395	129	Spun into ground near Ashford	20.08.44

Sqn Ldr M Cwynar. (Polish Institute).

Bibliography

Action Stations 9. Chris Ashworth. Patrick Stephens Ltd. 1985.

Fighter Squadrons of the RAF. John D Rawlings. Macdonald. 1969.

Mustang at War. Roger Freeman. Ian Allan Ltd. 1974.

History of the Polish Air Force. J B Cynk.

Poles Against the V1. Sqn Ldr B Arct.

British Military Airfields 1939-1945. David J Smith. Patrick Stephens Ltd. 1989.

Aces High. Christopher E Shores & Clive Williams. Grub Street, London. 1994.

The Doodlebugs. Norman Longmate. Hutchinson. 1981.

Buzz Bomb Diary. D Collyer/Kent Aviation Historical Research Society. 1994.

The Flying Bomb. Richard Anthony Young. Ian Allan Ltd. 1978.

This page and opposite: Extracts from the log book of Flt Lt M Cwynar, DFC, No 315 Sqn, RAF.

From: Group Captain F.W. Stannard,

HEADQUARTERS, A.E.A.F.,
KESTREL GROVE,
HIVE ROAD,
BUSHEY HEATH,
WATFORD, HERTS.

8th September, 1944.

FWS/DO.

Dear Cwynar,

My very heartiest congratulations on the award of the Distinguished Flying Cross which has been approved by the Air Commander-in-Chief today. I understand you have been with the Squadron since its formation and this, coupled with your fine record as an operational pilot, is indeed a fitting recommendation for the D.F.C., an award which we prize very highly.

I hoped to come down today to congratulate you personally but unfortunately I cannot get an aircraft. I hope, however, to be able to visit you in the very near future. Your Squadron certainly has put up a most magnificent show of which we are all extremely proud.

Looking forward to seeing you soon.

Yours ,

Frank Stannard.

Flight Lieutenant M. Cwynar, D.F.C.,
No. 315 Squadron,
Royal Air Force.

YEAR 1944		AIRCRAFT		PILOT, OR 1ST PILOT	2ND PILOT, PUPIL OR PASSENGER	DUTY (INCLUDING RESULTS AND REMARKS)	INSTR/CLOUD FLYING [Incl. in col. (1) to (10)]	
MONTH	DATE	Type	No.				DUAL	PILOT
						TOTALS BROUGHT FORWARD		
AUGUST	25	MUSTANG III.	G	SELF	NIL	84 ANTIDIVER PATROL		
	25.		R			TO COLTISHALL		
	25.		R			8 Dg EISCH. DOUFIGH. TO DENMARK		
	26.		V			TO NOEL HOLT		
	26.		4			FROM NORTH HOLT		
	27.		2			85 ANTIDIVER PATROL		
	29.		2			86 " "		
	30.		2			AIRCRAFT TEST		
					AUGUST	44		
					315 P. SQUADRON			
					1 SEPTEMBER 1944.			
					C. MYJQ W.			
					BREN = FN			
						TOTALS CARRIED FORWARD		

GODZIN OPERACYJNYCH : 50:40; 68:47:25 GRAND TOTAL [Cols. (1) to (10)] 1665 Hrs. 40 Mins.
BOJOWYCH : 25:50
DZIEŃM :

	SINGLE-ENGINE AIRCRAFT				MULTI-ENGINE AIRCRAFT							INSTR./CLOUD FLYING (Incl. in cols (1) to (10))	
	DAY		NIGHT		DAY		NIGHT			PASS-ENGER			
	DUAL	PILOT	DUAL	PILOT	DUAL	1ST PILOT	2ND PILOT	DUAL	1ST PILOT	2ND PILOT		DUAL	PILOT
	(1)	(2)	(3)	(4)	(5)	(6)	(7)	(8)	(9)	(10)	(11)	(12)	(13)
	79.50	1579.50											
		1.40											
		2.55											
		3.05											
		2.50											
		0.15											
		3.00											
		3.00											
		2.55											
		0.45											
		5.25											
		3.85											
		0.40											
		0.40											
		0.30											
		29.5'											
	79.50	1603.5T		1.35									

Headquarters,
No. 84 Group,
ROYAL AIR FORCE.

13th September, 1944.

Ref:- 84G/S.2211/1/2/1/Bear.

Dear Bonynet,

I want to extend to you my warm congratulations upon the award to you of the D.F.C. It was thoroughly well earned and deserved.

Wishing you good luck and further success,

Yours sincerely,

[signature]

L.O. BROWN,
Air Vice-Marshal, Commanding
No. 84 Group, R.A.F.

Flight Lieutenant K. CWYNAR, D.F.C.,
No. 315 (P) Squadron,
ROYAL AIR FORCE.

YEAR 1944		AIRCRAFT		PILOT, OR 1ST PILOT	2ND PILOT, PUPIL OR PASSENGER	DUTY (INCLUDING RESULTS AND REMARKS)
MONTH	DATE	Type	No.			
(5.)		—	—	—	—	TOTALS BROUGHT FORWARD
SEPTEMBER	2.	MUSTANG III	Z	SELF	nil	ANTIDIVER PATROL
	3.	"	Z			to 117 ESCORT HALIFAXES TO HOLLAND
	5.	"	Z			to 118 ARMED RECCO. KÖLN-HAMBURG AREA
	8.	"	Z			to 119 KLANGER. BREMEN-HANNOVER.
	9.	"	U			AIRCRAFT TEST
	10.	"	Z			to 120 ARMED RECCO. LEEUWARDEN HOLLAND HANNOVER AR.
	11.	"	Z			to 121 ESCORT 150 LANCASTERS TO KNUR
	12.	"	Z			132 ESCORT 150 HALIFAX TO HANNOVER.
	13.	"	Z			TO MENDON
	1(7).	"	Z			ESCORT 3 DAKOTA TO PARIS
	24.	"	Z			to 123 ESCORT 100 HALIFAX TO DINA BRZLIC
	24.		1			AIRCRAFT TEST
	25.		U			TO NORIHOLT
	25.		U			FROM NORIHOLT
					SEPTEMBER 1944	
					315 (P) SQUADRON	
					26.9.1944.	
					CWYNAR	
					R.A.F. BRENZE 77	
					TOTALS CARRIED FORWARD	

GODZIN OPERACYJNYCH 50'40. RB. 4725. GRAND TOTAL [Cols. (1) to (10)] 169H 45 Hrs. Mins.
BOJOWYCH - 277.40
RAZEM - 352.00

This page and following four pages: Extracts from the log book of Sqn Ldr P H Thompson, DFC, who was the CO of No 129 (Mysore) Sqn, RAF, at Brenzett ALG from July 1944, and remained with the squadron until April 1945.

F.L.S. MILFIELD - 129 (MYSORE) SQUADRON - FORD - BRENZETT.

YEAR 1944		AIRCRAFT		PILOT, OR 1ST PILOT	2ND PILOT, PUPIL OR PASSENGER	DUTY (INCLUDING RESULTS AND REMARKS)	SINGLE-ENGINE DAY Pilot	NIGHT Pilot	OPS. PRES. TOUR
MONTH	DATE	Type	No.						
						TOTALS BROUGHT FORWARD	17.05	2.50 21.55	
JULY	8	MUSTANG III	DV. H	SELF	—	LOCAL	.45		.30
	9	MUSTANG III	DV. H	SELF	—	FORD - BRENZETT	.30		
	11	MUSTANG III	DV. H	SELF	—	DIVER PATROL	2.00		1.00
	12	MUSTANG III	DV. H	SELF	—	DIVER PATROL	1.30		.45
	15	AUSTER III	NK.126	SELF	F/O MASON	LOCAL	1.45		
	15	MUSTANG III	DV. H	SELF	—	WEATHER TEST	1.10		
	16	MUSTANG III	DV. H	SELF	—	DIVER PATROL	1.30		.45
	16	AUSTER III	NK 126	SELF	F/O MASON	LOCAL	.30		
	18	MUSTANG III	DV. H	SELF	—	PRACTICE FLYING	1.00		
	19	MUSTANG III	DV. H	SELF	—	DIVER PATROL	1.10		.35
	20	MUSTANG III	DV. H	SELF	—	DIVER PATROL	2.10		1.05
	23	MUSTANG III	DU. H	SELF	—	DIVER PATROL	1.45		.50
	28	MUSTANG III	DV. H	SELF	—	DIVER PATROL	2.05		1.05
	30	MUSTANG III	DV. H	SELF	—	DIVER - PATROL	2.20		1.10
	31	MUSTANG III	DV. H	SELF	—	DIVER PATROL	2.20	1 DIVER DESTROYED. .6	.10

AUSTER.

MUSTANG

PREVIOUS OPS. 596.35
OPS PRES. TOUR. 8.25

SUMMARY FOR JULY. 1944.	MUSTANG	20.15		
129 (MYSORE) SQDN.	AUSTER	1.5		22.25
3 August 1944	MAGISTER	.55		
[signature] S/LDR				

TOTALS CARRIED FORWARD 20.25 1200. .35 2.50 21.55 .30

GRAND TOTAL [Cols. (1) to (10)] 131.7 Hrs. 15 Mins.

70

129 (MYSORE) SQDN.   BRENZETT.

YEAR 1944		AIRCRAFT		PILOT, OR 1ST PILOT	2ND PILOT, PUPIL OR PASSENGER	DUTY (INCLUDING RESULTS AND REMARKS)	SINGLE-ENGINE AIRCRAFT			MULTI-ENGINE AIRCRAFT							OPS	
MONTH	DATE	Type	No.				DAY Dual	DAY Pilot	NIGHT Dual	NIGHT Pilot	DAY Dual	DAY 1st Pilot	DAY 2nd Pilot	NIGHT Dual	NIGHT 1st Pilot	NIGHT 2nd Pilot	OPS	P.Tour
AUG.	4	—	—	—	—	Totals Brought Forward		1200.35	2.50	21.25		.30						8.26
	4	MUSTANG III	DV. H	SELF	—	DIVER PATROL		1.30										.30
	5	MUSTANG III	DN. H	SELF	—	DIVER PATROL		55										.45
	5	MUSTANG III	DV. H	SELF	—	DIVER PATROL GF. 1		1.20										.50
	7	MUSTANG III	DV. H	SELF	—	DIVER PATROL		2.30										—
	11	MUSTANG III	DV. H	SELF	—	LOCAL		.30										—
	15	MUSTANG III	DV. H	SELF	—	DIVER PATROL		1.50										.40
	17	MUSTANG III	DV. H	SELF	—	✳ RANGER		1.50			12 A/C TO PARIS VIA DUNKIRK BUT OVER 10/10THS. FLAK AT DUNGENESS								1.50
	18	MUSTANG III	DV. H	SELF	—	✳ RANGER		1.50			12 A/C BEAVAIS - SOISSONS - LILLE GRAVELINES 4/10THS - NO E/A.								1.50
	18	MUSTANG III	DV. H	SELF	—	A/E TEST		.20										
	23	MUSTANG III	DV. H	SELF	—	LOCAL AND X COUNTRY		3.15										
	26	MUSTANG III	DV. H	SELF	—	✳ ARMED RECCE		1.30			12 A/C LOOKING FOR TARGETS IN GHENT - LILLE AREA. N.M.S								1.30
	26	MUSTANG III	DV. H	SELF	—	LOCAL		.30				.30						
						SUMMARY FOR AUGUST 1944 MUSTANG 129 (MYSORE) SQUADRON. [st] September 1944.		14.50											
								125										

GRAND TOTAL (Cols. (1) to (10))
1335 Hrs. 05 Mins.

TOTALS CARRIED FORWARD: | 1218.25 | 2.50 | 21.25 | | .30 | | | | | | | 16.20

129 (MYSORE) SQUADRON - BRENZETT

YEAR 1944 Month / Date	AIRCRAFT Type	No.	PILOT, OR 1ST PILOT	2ND PILOT, PUPIL OR PASSENGER	DUTY (INCLUDING RESULTS AND REMARKS)	SE DAY Pilot	SE NIGHT Pilot	ME DAY 1st Pilot	ME DAY 2nd Pilot	ME NIGHT	O/S Pass. Engine
					TOTALS BROUGHT FORWARD	10.25 12/6.25	2.50 21.25	.30		2.50 22.25	16.20
SEPT 1	MUSTANG	DV. H	SELF	—	DIVER PATROL	1.55			1 DIVER DESTROYED		.40
SEPT 5	MUSTANG	DV. H	SELF	※	ARMED RECCE — To ARNHEM - ELST 2MT AT VIANEN DESTROYED. PETROL TRAIN AT ELST COMPLETELY WRITTEN OFF TOTAL 12 M.T. PLENTY OF L.A.A.	2.25					2.25
5	MUSTANG	DV. H	SELF	※	ARMED RECCE — TRIED TO FIND MT. PARK AT NIJMEGAN. BUT IT WAS TOO DARK.	2.00	1.00		PARK AT NIJMEGAN 2.00		2.00
6	MUSTANG	DV. H	SELF	—	LANDED NEWCHURCH	.10					
6	MUSTANG	DV. H	SELF	※	FROM NEWCHURCH. ESCORT TO LANCASTERS — To EMDEN. VERY GOOD BOMBING SOME H.A.A. AT 18,000 - NO E/A. 10/10 THS AT 19,000'	3.10					3.10
13	MUSTANG	DV. H	SELF	—	To HENDON — RATHER FUN IN 10/10THS AT 0'	1.00					
13	MUSTANG	DV. H	SELF	—	To LE BOURGET — ESCORT MR DUFF COOPER TO PARIS	3.15					
14	MUSTANG	DV. H	SELF	※	ESCORT 1ST AIRBOURNE — PARIS LOOKED JUST THE SAME!! ANTI-FLAK FOR GLIDERS ETC BUT HUN GUNNERS KEPT VERY QUIET THOUSANDS OF A/C - MAGNIFICENT!!	3.50					3.50
18	MUSTANG	DV. H	SELF	—	To CHIVENOR.	1.00					—
18	MUSTANG	DV. H	SELF	—	FROM CHIVENOR.	1.00					
20	MUSTANG	DV. H	SELF	※	ESCORT TO STIRLINGS — DROPPING SUPPLIES TO PARATROOPS AT ARNHEM. FILTHY WEATHER. (SOME L.A.A OTHERWISE UNEVENTFUL	2.45					2.45
25	MUSTANG	DV. H	SELF	※	ESCORT TO BOSTONS AND MITCHELLS — BOMBING ARNHEM. BIG DOG FIGHT WITH 50+ FW190s AND ME109s. MY LONG RANGE TANKS WOULD NOT DROP! MOST ANNOYING BECAUSE I HAD A FW190 STONE COLD. MY No2 F/Lt PARKER SHOT IT DOWN. LOST MYNARD AND HUMPHRIES BOTH BALED OUT. SQUADRON SCORE 4-0	2.45					2.45
					TOTALS CARRIED FORWARD	13.14 12/9.40	2.50 22.25			4-0	33.55

GRAND TOTAL [Cols. (1) to (10)] 1361 Hrs. 20 Mins.

129 (MYSORE) SQDN. ~ BRENZETT.

YEAR 1944 Date	Aircraft Type	No.	Pilot, or 1st Pilot	2nd Pilot, Pupil or Passenger	Duty (Including Results and Remarks)	Single-Engine Day Dual	Single-Engine Day Pilot	Single-Engine Night Dual	Single-Engine Night Pilot	Multi Day Dual	Multi Day 1st Pilot	Multi Day 2nd Pilot	Multi Night 1st Pilot	Multi Night 2nd Pilot	OPS	Instr/Cloud Flying Dual	Pilot
					TOTALS BROUGHT FORWARD	.25	1244.40	2.50	22.25		.30				33.55		
SEPT 26	MUSTANG	DV. H	SELF	—	※ ESCORT TO D.C.3s — 200+ DAKOTAS LANDED AT A.L.G 3 JUST LIKE CLOCK- WORK. 3/10THS H400.		3.45								3.45		
28	MUSTANG	DV. H	SELF	—	A/E TEST		.30										
29	MUSTANG	DV. H	SELF	—	A/E TEST		.30										
30	MUSTANG	DV. H	SELF	—	※ ESCORT TO LANCASTERS — 100 LANCS BOMBING STACK/CRADE OIL PLANT IN RUHR. ABOVE 10/10THS H400.		2.50								2.50		
	MUSTANG				TOTAL OPS. AREA TOUR		32.50		1.00						40.30		
					SUMMARY FOR SEPT. 1944 129 (MYSORE) SQDN. BRENZETT. 1st October 1944. [signature] S/L.									.40			
OCT 2	MUSTANG	DV. H	SELF	—	※ SWEEP — OSNABRUCK- MUNSTER AREA IN SUPPORT OF MITCHELLS. NO ACTIVITY		3.00								3.00		
3	AUSTER	MK299	SELF	F/L MASON	LOCAL		.25										
3	MUSTANG	DV. Z	SELF	—	NIGHT FORMATION				.40								
4	MUSTANG	DV. H	SELF	—	PRACTICE CLOUD FLYING		1.10										
6	MUSTANG	DV. H	SELF	—	※ WING SWEEP — LEADING WING IN SWEEP ROUND RHUR VIA KOLN - MUNSTER N.A.		3.15								3.00		
					TOTALS CARRIED FORWARD	.05	1260.05	2.50	23.05						46.30		

GRAND TOTAL [Cols. (1) to (10)] 1376 Hrs. 45 Mins.

129 (MYSORE) SQUADRON - ANDREWS FIELD.

YEAR 1944 MONTH	DATE	AIRCRAFT Type	No.	PILOT, OR 1ST PILOT	2ND PILOT, PUPIL OR PASSENGER	DUTY (INCLUDING RESULTS AND REMARKS)				
						TOTALS BROUGHT FORWARD				
OCT	7	MUSTANG	DV. H	SELF	-	ESCORT TO LANCASTERS				
	10	MUSTANG	DV. H	SELF	-	MOVE TO ANDREWS FIELD				
	13	MUSTANG	DV. H	SELF	-	ESCORT TO MITCHELLS				
	14	MUSTANG	DV. H	SELF	-	ESCORT TO LANCASTERS				
	18	MUSTANG	DV. H.	SELF	-	ESCORT TO LANCASTERS				
	20	MUSTANG	DV. H	SELF		TO MILFIELD AND RETURN				
	26	MUSTANG	DV. H	SELF		A/E TEST.				
	27	MUSTANG	DV. H	SELF		NIGHT FLYING				
	30	MUSTANG	DV. H	SELF		ESCORT TO LANCASTERS				

Engine columns (Single-Engine / Multi-Engine / OPS):

DATE	DUTY	SINGLE-ENGINE Day Dual	SINGLE-ENGINE Day Pilot	SINGLE-ENGINE Night Dual	SINGLE-ENGINE Night Pilot	MULTI-ENGINE remarks	OPS hours
	TOTALS BROUGHT FORWARD	1/25 1/260.05	2.50	23.05			46.30
7	ESCORT TO LANCASTERS	4.35				13 LANCS. WITH 12.000 lbs. BLEW UP. DAM AT KEMBS. FLAK !!!	4.35
10	MOVE TO ANDREWS FIELD	1.10					
13	ESCORT TO MITCHELLS	2.45				MITCHELLS COULD NOT EVEN FIND THE TARGET AT UTRECHT. N.A.	2.45
14	ESCORT TO LANCASTERS	3.30				EXIT DUISBERG !! 1000 LANCS ON A MAGNIFICIENT PRANG H.A.A. N.A.	3.30
18	ESCORT TO LANCASTERS	3.45				COCK-UP 120 LANCS TO BONN OVER 10/10THS. LOST WING AND P/O BERTRAND	3.45
20	TO MILFIELD AND RETURN	3.00					
26	A/E TEST.	.45					
27	NIGHT FLYING	.50					
30	ESCORT TO LANCASTERS	2.40				100 LANCS BOMBING S.W. KÖLN THROUGH 10/10THS. N.A.	2.40

SUMMARY FOR OCTOBER. MUSTANG
129 (MYSORE) SQUADRON AUST.
2nd November 1944
[signature]

	SINGLE-ENGINE Day Dual	SINGLE-ENGINE Day Pilot	NIGHT	OPS
	29.25		1.30	63.45
	.25			

GRAND TOTAL [Cols. (1) to (10)] TOTALS CARRIED FORWARD

		Pilot					
	1/25	1/262	.15	2.50	23.55		63.45

GRAND TOTAL [Cols. (1) to (10)]
1400 Hrs. 25 Mins.

74